"Phil's writing feels like a friend holding you [ ] hardest struggles: being hurt by another person. His biblical, step-by-step advice will help you overcome betrayal and emerge with confidence. This book is the answer for so many people who need healing."

—**Rachel Cruze,** #1 *New York Times* bestselling author and host of *The Rachel Cruze Show*

"I just returned from a conference where people were standing in line to get *Beyond Betrayal*. My friend Phil Waldrep has hit a nerve. It's quite impossible to get all the way through life without feeling the anguish of betrayal. And if perchance it hasn't happened to you yet, you know and love someone who is going through this dark place right now. In *Beyond Betrayal*, Phil offers clear, compassionate, Christlike counsel that will help you find your way through these difficult days and discover that there truly is life beyond betrayal."

—**Dr. David Jeremiah,** founder and president of Turning Point Ministries, senior pastor, Shadow Mountain Community Church, El Cajon, CA

"*Beyond Betrayal* is a practical guide for walking through the pain of betrayal, learning to trust again, and letting Jesus into the pain to heal and redeem it."

—**Christine Caine,** bestselling author, founder of A21 and Propel Women

"I believe we have all experienced types of betrayal in our lives in some way. From friends who break promises, to spouses who betray vows, or business partners embezzling funds—the result of betrayal is often bitterness. As my friend Phil Waldrep shares in this powerful book, you can find freedom from your hurts and healing in the midst of pain."

—**Candace Cameron Bure,** actress, producer, *New York Times* bestselling author

"We have so little language for life after betrayal. I've learned so much from Phil Waldrep and his gentle wisdom for those of us who want to move on but don't know how."

—**Kate Bowler,** *New York Times* bestselling author of
Everything Happens for a Reason and Other Lies I've Loved

"If you've ever been betrayed by anyone for any reason, this is the resource you've been looking for. *Beyond Betrayal* offers a step-by-step path to freedom from the hurt, fear, anger, distrust, guilt, bitterness, and regret that inevitably follow the initial shock of a betrayal. Sharing a depth of wisdom gained only through painful personal experience, Phil Waldrep guides you toward hope and healing, even as he points again and again to the One who makes all things new. You won't find pat answers or easy solutions here—only honest and effective counsel from a compassionate friend who wants to help you live again. A wonderful, powerful book."

—**Liz Curtis Higgs,** bestselling author of *Bad Girls of the Bible*

"I have known Phil Waldrep for years. He is one of the nicest people you'd ever want to meet and even he was betrayed. In this book Phil will show you how to get through betrayal without becoming bitter and broken."

—**Mark Lowry,** singer, author, humorist, and songwriter of the
Christmas classic "Mary, Did You Know?"

"Phil Waldrep is one of the kindest, most genuine men I know. His story proves that God absolutely can heal our deepest emotional wounds, we can choose redemption over retribution, and scars can morph into the loveliest kind of beauty marks."

—**Lisa Harper,** bestselling author and Bible teacher

"Betrayal can leave a lifelong sting, and yet we have the opportunity to transform how we feel, think, and remember what happened to us. Phil Waldrep is a trusted guide through these challenging waters."

—**Jay and Katherine Wolf,** bestselling authors
and founders of Hope Heals

"Betrayal hurts, but bitterness hurts us even more. That's why I appreciate Phil Waldrep so much. He not only takes you along on his own personal journey of betrayal, but he gives spiritual guidance to help you stand tall on the other side without harboring resentment. This is a great resource for anyone who is in the hard middle of a broken relationship."

—**Jennifer Rothschild,** author of *Lessons I Learned in the Dark,* founder of Fresh Grounded Faith events and 4:13 Podcast

"I have great respect for Phil Waldrep as a pastor and a friend. In this book he becomes our mentor, walking us through the painful mazes of betrayal and heartache. He doesn't pull any punches—if you have been broken by betrayal, you will find a wise and compassionate friend who will guide you to a place of peace and freedom in Christ."

—**Sheila Walsh,** bestselling author of *It's Ok Not to Be Ok*

"Phil Waldrep has walked through betrayal and come out on the other side of the pain with rich insights, healing words, and strategies for overcoming such heartache. His teaching and tactics will revolutionize your life and set you free."

—**Margaret Feinberg,** author of *Taste and See* and host of *The Joycast* podcast

"Unfortunately, we have all dealt with the issue of betrayal, and I can tell you from personal experience that it's one of the hardest wounds to heal. Through biblical narratives and his own personal story, Phil invites the reader to come to the place of peace that he has found. We can't live in resentment and expect to know the joyful life that Jesus has promised, and I'm grateful for these words because they speak to the freedom on the other side of forgiveness."

—**Angie Smith,** bestselling author

BEYOND BETRAYAL

PHIL WALDREP

HARVEST HOUSE PUBLISHERS
EUGENE, OREGON

Cover design by Faceout Studio

Front cover photo © deckorator / Shutterstock

Published in association with The Christopher Ferebee Agency. [CC1]

Beyond Betrayal
Copyright © 2020 by Phil Waldrep
Published by Harvest House Publishers
Eugene, Oregon 97408
www.harvesthousepublishers.com

ISBN 978-0-7369-7877-4 (pbk)
ISBN 978-0-7369-7878-1 (eBook)

Library of Congress Cataloging-in-Publication Data

Names: Waldrep, Phil, author.
Title: Beyond betrayal : overcome past hurts and begin to trust again / Phil Waldrep.
Description: Eugene : Harvest House Publishers, 2020. |
Identifiers: LCCN 2019028493 (print) | LCCN 2019028494 (ebook) | ISBN 9780736978774 (trade paperback) | ISBN 9780736978781 (ebook)
Subjects: LCSH: Forgiveness--Religious aspects--Christianity. | Betrayal.
Classification: LCC BV4647.F55 W35 2020 (print) | LCC BV4647.F55 (ebook) | DDC 248.8/6--dc23
LC record available at https://lccn.loc.gov/2019028493
LC ebook record available at https://lccn.loc.gov/2019028494

Printed in the United States of America
19 20 21 22 23 24 25 26 27 / BP-GL / 10 9 8 7 6 5 4 3 2 1

CONTENTS

For Emory Ann, Zoe, Bryce, and Caleb

FOREWORD

You have to know how I mean it:

I am sorry.

I am sorry for the pain that's been burning a searing hole out the side of your heart, that's scorched your days and profaned your moments with the lingering stench of betrayal.

I am sorry your trust wasn't prized—and a hard-won bit of you was painfully lost.

I am sorry for what now is, that should never have been.

You didn't sign up for this.

You didn't sign up to have your trust torched, your kindness kindled into flame, your security to go up in smoke. You didn't sign up to be duped and deluded, used and abused, and you didn't for one moment expect anyone to play Judas and play false with the story of your life.

They got what they wanted, and you got shafted in ways you never planned. They got the upper hand, and you got taken advantage of. They got what wasn't theirs, and you got what you never wanted.

Sometimes: The gravest wrong isn't how they betrayed you, but how you ever trusted them.

Sometimes: Betrayal feels like holding hands with what twisted into a trap that chewed up and spit out part of your heart.

Sometimes: An enemy's frontal assault hurts less than the backstabbing of a friend.

And now, you're desperate for a sign that points the way out of this mess.

This moment, these hopeful pages, the transparent story you will find in these life-transforming pages, is a sign from God for you, a roadmap out of where you never expected to be.

You get to choose to trust others again, you get to choose to forgive, you get to choose the bravest story. You get to rise courageously because: Forgiveness only happens where a death has happened.

Forgiveness only happens where hope has died, expectations have died, plans have died, reputation has died, fairness has died, dreams have died.

You get to be brave in the face of betrayal and choose: If you don't die to something so you can forgive someone, it's your own quality of life and very soul that begins to die.

There is never any forgiveness without someone getting to pay for it. There is no forgiveness without demanding the cost or paying the cost.

That is always the choice you make every day when you look in the mirror: Either I can pay for the wrong, or I can try to make the betrayer pay for it.

There is always the choice: I can pay the price—and die to my anger. I can pay the price—and die to my revenge. I can pay the price—and die to my desire to get even and give even the betrayer the grace even I have been given.

There is never any forgiveness without someone giving up something to pay for it. There is no forgiveness without demanding the cost—or paying the cost.

And the thing is:

Every time you try to make someone pay, they are the ones who get to be in charge of your life.

When you try to make someone pay, they dominate your thoughts, they take control of your energy, they seize your heart and mind and time.

When you hold your forgiveness ransom until someone pays you back and earns your love, you're the one whose quality of life gets poorer and poorer.

Time is nonrefundable and every betrayal has already stolen so much from you—you can't betray your own soul by spending another moment on animosity. The betrayal wounded you once. Bitterness now doesn't get to multiply the wounds.

You know it: Wishing another ill will only makes you ill.

You believe it: Everyone has been betrayed. But betrayal doesn't get to destroy your trust in everyone. Just because every betrayal begins with trust doesn't mean every betrayal has to end with cynicism.

You choose it: Wisdom is different than cynicism.

Whatever that betrayal took from you, it doesn't get to take every relationship from you.

You get to turn the rare gift of these vulnerable pages that hold life-giving healing and radical freedom, and you get to turn to the face in the mirror and ask:

How can I not pass on the cup of grace that I have drunk so deeply from?

How can I refuse anyone the mercy that I have needed to stay alive?

How can I weigh what anyone has done against me as heavier and what Jesus has done for me as far lighter?

Live forgiving—to live forgiven.

Sit long with the courageous truth of Phil Waldrep's hard-earned cruciform wisdom and gaze long with him on the cross: Remember what Jesus has done for you, and you will remember how to forgive.

Forgiveness is hard only when we forget what Jesus has done for us and remember only what has been done against us.

You can't know how sorry I am for the pain you've experienced—and you have to know how the lifeline of these pages will meet you in that pain and show you how to experience the freedom you were always meant for.

Even now: Trust that you can trust again.

Ann Voskamp
from her farm on a warm autumn day, 2019,
author of the *New York Times* bestsellers *The Broken Way* and *One Thousand Gifts*

INNOCENCE

It is easier to forgive an enemy than a friend.

—William Blake

It always seems to come out of nowhere. One moment the birds are singing, the sun is shining, and life is good.

Then, like the strike of a bolt of lightning, our world is turned upside down.

You discover that everything you thought, believed, and assumed about someone close to you is wrong—*false*, in fact. The person you trusted, the one you did life or family or business with, is a liar and a sham.

How do you know? Because that person betrayed you.

You discover a business partner has been embezzling from you for years or one day just up and announces he's leaving to start his own company (with your trade secrets!) and has left you deeply in debt.

The spouse that said they loved you with all their heart and promised to be faithful "until death do us part" is having an affair with another person.

The friend you trusted to invest your retirement money embezzled it and spent it on extravagant living. As you dig deeper you discover he's been running a Ponzi scheme for years.

You find out a coworker and friend revealed personal secrets about you to get a promotion instead of you.

Yeah, *that person.* The person who, if possible, you would just as soon never see or speak to again.

You gave them your trust and confided in them—and they used that to pull the wool over your eyes. They deceived you and may even have robbed you.

Now, they don't care. To them, it is no big deal.

You want an explanation. They don't offer one. If they do, it's your fault, not theirs. You want to hear: "I am sorry." But if you do, you know they don't mean it.

What is worse is family members or mutual friends seem to care more about them than you. They certainly aren't rallying to your side.

You scream, "Why me?"

The night it happened, you cried until your pillow was as soggy as a blanket left out in the rain.

Everywhere you look you are reminded of two things: *you were betrayed,* and *you were betrayable.*

How could I have been such a fool?

Every time someone looks at you, you're sure they're thinking,

I don't know of any other pain in life that is worse than being betrayed by someone close to you. It changes everything.

There goes a person who was gullible enough to put their trust in a traitor. How naïve can a person be?

You wonder how you'll ever be able to trust anyone again.

Honestly, I don't know of any other pain in life that is worse than being betrayed by someone close to you. It changes everything. After such an experience, the world is simply a different place—one far darker and crueler than you ever thought possible before.

Sure, you've watched others have painful, life-changing experiences, but there was always an explanation. Your aunt and uncle lost their home because of a tornado or a hurricane.

But no one can control the weather. Right?

The doctor told a close friend that she has ALS. She certainly doesn't deserve it, but there was nothing anyone could do to prevent it.

A neighbor lost his job because the company was moving overseas. It's the fault of those selfish politicians! What are we supposed to do?

Painful? *Sure.*

Life-changing? *Absolutely.*

But at least there was a reason for their pain. It was all beyond their control or the control of people they loved. *No one hurt them intentionally. It was just happenstance.*

But your pain? *That is different.*

In your case, someone you trusted deliberately used you, hurt you, robbed you, and left you emotionally destitute. Now you want answers.

Why? What did I do to deserve this?

How could anyone abuse your emotions and destroy your dreams so casually? Why would anyone convince you of one thing and do the opposite? If they didn't want to live or work with you, then why didn't they tell you the truth instead of acting like they loved you and then doing all that other stuff behind your back?

How are you going to face tomorrow?

If you are like most people who have faced betrayal, you've already answered that one. Your first instinct is to build four walls around your heart, refuse to let anyone inside, and never be vulnerable again. You want an ironclad guarantee that you will never experience pain and hurt at this level for the rest of your life.

Life might not be as fun behind four walls, but at least it won't be so painful. Let me tell you from experience: *That's no way to live.*

Though betrayal can feel like the end—and it is the end of some things—it doesn't have to be the end of you. It doesn't have to color every relationship you have for the rest of your life. It doesn't mean God has turned His back on you or is punishing you for something you've done (or didn't do).

I promise you, the sun will shine again in your life. You can trust again, though that may be hard to fathom with the way you feel right now.

How do I know?

Because I have been betrayed. Deeply betrayed. For me, it was a close friend and colleague.

It affected my life emotionally, financially, and spiritually. It caused me to withdraw from relationships and vow never to trust again.

It changed the way I treated and interacted with people.

It took years to process what happened and acknowledge that it changed me.

Whether it has been a recent wound that hurts to mention or a betrayal years ago that you never addressed, I'd like to show you the path to recovery.

Today, as a result, I am stronger, better, and happier that I have ever been. Believe me, there is hope!

So, I am inviting you to allow me to walk with you through the pain and emotions that you are feeling. Whether it has been a recent wound that hurts to mention or a betrayal years ago that you never addressed, I'd like to show you the path to recovery.

It will take some time, but you will get there.

In sharing openly and honestly with you, my prayer is that it won't take you as much time as it took me. My hope is that, in these pages, I can meet you where you are—whether you are in the pit of the pain the betrayal caused or if it has been a few years since it occurred, we can work together towards a better day for you.

I will admit that I don't know everything about recovering from betrayal, but I do know a few things. I have walked through betrayal and come out on the other side of pain. One of the things I can tell you now is that it is hard to climb out of this pit alone. That is why I want to answer a few questions you are asking to help you process your feelings—or at least I want to get you started.

But I can promise that, if you start the journey, someday—not tomorrow or the next, but one day—the birds will be singing and the sun will be shining again, and life will be good.

At least that was my experience. And I have seen it happen for others who I have walked through betrayal with as a friend, confidante, and sometimes a minister. I believe the same can happen for you.

But before we get too much further, let me share what happened to me. My credentials for talking about this aren't because I have a degree in psychology or have developed a counseling program to help others.

What I've learned and share here is from personal experience, both from my story and the stories of other people who faced betrayal.

My hope is that my story and the stories of others will help you understand your story.

So, before we talk about anything else, let me tell you what happened to me as I remember it.

....

One

BETRAYAL

Even my close friend in whom I trusted,
who ate my bread, has lifted his heel against me.

—Psalm 41:9

I remember it being a beautiful, sunny Tuesday morning. The birds were singing outside my office window and it was one of those days in the South when the sun seems to shine out of everything.

I was at the office looking forward to a day of catch-up. That is a day when I don't schedule meetings, but try to answer mail, respond to emails, and plan for the months ahead. I intentionally schedule these days to prevent me from getting behind in my commitments. This day had a higher stack of paperwork than normal.

On days like that, I try to avoid phone conversations and any unexpected guests who might happen to drop by. This day, in particular, I needed time to focus and not be distracted. Many of the items needing my attention required a great deal of thought.

Having been out of town for several days, I knew I would have a full day of it. I communicated my wishes not to be disturbed to my secretary who faithfully acts as my gatekeeper.

So I was surprised when she buzzed my office to tell me that I had visitors. I didn't want to be rude, but I asked if she could explain to them that I wasn't available and, if possible, find a time to schedule an appointment.

She said, "Well, I don't know if I can do that. They appear to be important people."

"Do you know them?" I asked, wondering if it was a friend or one of our employees having a personal crisis.

"No, but I think they are important," she said again with a seriousness I rarely heard in her voice. "They are wearing suits and stated they are with the federal government. They declined to give their names, but stressed it was urgent that they see you."

Was I in some kind of trouble? I asked my secretary to bring them to my office. Moments later, she did.

I didn't recognize either man, but I knew this wasn't a prank. These men were on official business. One of them closed my office door behind him as he entered, giving a quick look up and down the hall before he did.

I politely introduced myself, expecting them to do the same. Instead of telling me their names, they asked if anyone else was in my office or could hear our conversation.

"No, there isn't," I answered.

"Good," the older of the two said as he reached for his jacket pocket.

They flashed badges concealed in small black wallets—just like on some detective show—and told me their names. They represented two different federal law enforcement agencies that were working together on an investigation.

"I appreciate your service to our country," I responded, expecting one of them to tell me that he interacted at some point with our ministry and they had just stopped by to say hello. That, at least, was what I was hoping. "Won't you have a seat?" I motioned to two chairs nearby. I returned to my chair behind my desk. We all sat down.

Once seated, they leaned forward. The older gentleman continued, taking a low, confidential tone. "Mr. Waldrep, we need to ask you a few questions."

Now I knew it was serious. Anyone who grew up, as I did, watching those same detective shows, knows a suspect is in trouble when the investigator just "needs to ask you a few questions."

My heart was pounding. Had someone in my family done something? One of our employees? *Me?*

In my heart, I knew there was nothing illegal in my life. But I began to wonder. *What if someone was trying to frame me? What for? What will I do? How can I prove my innocence?*

"Before we ask you any questions, we must first swear you to secrecy. What we are about to share cannot be discussed with your wife, your family, or your friends—and it certainly cannot be mentioned to any member of your staff."

The agent went on to explain that breaking that code of silence could jeopardize informants, law enforcement officers, and a major federal investigation.

"Sir, do you fully understand the seriousness of our visit?" he asked.

"Yes, sir," I said as the blood drained from my face.

"Good."

Then, for the next hour, the investigators shared what they were investigating: a money-laundering group in a major city. At this point, they were not sure how many people were involved or who they were.

Money laundering, they explained, was a way criminals convert their ill-gotten gains into cash they can spend. Al Capone wasn't arrested for selling drugs or for murder, but for tax evasion. He had no way to account for the large sums of money that were passing through his hands because he hadn't correctly "laundered" it.

If a major drug lord takes large sums of money and puts it into a bank account, the bank and police will wonder how he got it. That, in turn, launches an investigation and makes it easy to catch them (just as happened with Capone).

If, on the other hand, the criminal can mix that money with income from a legitimate business or the sale of something like a parcel of real estate, law enforcement can't trace the money as easily. Even if a customer never walks through the door of their company, that money looks more legitimate on a bank register.

But it is usually more complicated than that. More experienced criminals will filter the money through several people or businesses along the way, mixing good money with bad, making it even more difficult to determine which was which. The more they do that, the harder it is to prove in court that the money came from illegal activities.

"So, how does your investigation lead you to me?" I asked.

"Well, sir, someone you know has a relative under investigation." The agent quickly added that my friend's relative was not under indictment, just one of the many people they were look-ing into. He may, in fact, have nothing to do with the laundering at all. And, at this point, it seemed certain to me that my friend was completely clueless about what his relative might be doing.

"What do you need from me?" I wondered aloud.

They each removed a small notebook from their pockets. One read through a list of questions he had written while the other took notes on my answers.

Most of the questions were general. I had limited knowledge of my friend's relative, so I couldn't help as much as they thought. Then they began to ask detailed questions about my employees and some additional friends. It didn't take me long to realize that my friend was part of the investigation as well as his relative.

When I asked if he was, they replied, "Sir, as we said earlier, there are many people currently under investigation. In a money-laundering investigation, we have to eliminate the innocent in order to find the guilty."

After they had worked through their list of questions, one of them asked me if I would be willing to assist them in obtaining additional information. They could tell I was reluctant to partic-ipate. "It would help us clear your friend and his relative more quickly, if they're not guilty," they offered.

That made sense. Since I felt sure he was innocent, I agreed to help in any way I could.

Before leaving, they again pressed the importance of absolute confidentiality. They explained the information they needed and how I would convey it to them without anyone else suspecting I was passing information on to law enforcement.

All I can share at this point, even years later, is that they had some pretty ingenious ways to pass information along.

Then they gave me a list of things they needed to know, such as: Where would my friend and his relative be spending the holidays? Have they purchased anything new or expensive? Are they planning any major vacations or trips in the future? And so on.

Looking back, most of the information seemed routine, and I'm not sure how vital it really was. I think it was partly testing my honesty and partly saving them time researching mundane details.

Clearing a Friend

That conversation started three months of torture for me. I couldn't tell anyone, even my wife, about anything they were doing or that I was doing for them. It was extremely isolating.

The minute they walked out the door, of course, the questions from my staff started. They wanted to know who the men were and why they had come.

The investigators gave me an alibi. I was to say they were doing a background check on a friend who worked at NASA in nearby Huntsville, Alabama, that had requested a higher security clearance, something that happens quite often in our area.

So that's what I told them. Even though it was for a good cause, now I was getting mired in the falseness.

It wasn't very long until my wife wanted to know what was bothering me. She particularly wanted to know why I was quieter in the evenings than usual. (If you know me, you know I tend to be a talker.) I imagine some mysterious disappearances during the day didn't help. But keeping something so personal from my wife felt so wrong.

Each time I gave a "reasonable" explanation. Fortunately for me, my wife accepted it and conveyed her love and trust.

But that wasn't the worst of it. Soon the worrying settled in. What if my friend and his relative *were* involved? What if some mob boss was having me watched because he suspected I was helping the authorities? Would he threaten me or harm my family for assisting?

Granted, that may be the norm for law enforcement agents and their families, but for me, it wasn't. I was suddenly in some film noir from the forties and started looking everywhere with suspicion. I started doing much more than just looking both ways before crossing the street. I began looking at every parked car expecting to see two thugs sitting in it and watching me pass by.

But nothing like that happened. I survived the entire investigation unscathed except for a little psychological wear and tear. Truth be told, I wasn't as big a player as I thought at the time.

Three months later, I had my final meeting with one of the investigators. He was upbeat and happy. He informed me that my friend and his relative, along with those associated with them, were all cleared of involvement. In fact, the investigation resulted in the arrests of people in a city on the other side of the country far from the original point of investigation.

He thanked me for my assistance and got up to leave. I was relieved. My life was about to return to normal.

Or so I thought.

As the agent approached the door, he stopped, turned, and came back to me. His smile was gone. He suddenly looked as serious as he had at our first meeting.

"Mr. Waldrep, I didn't know you before this investigation, but I believe you are a good man with a good heart. What I am about to tell you isn't something we usually share, but I think you deserve to know."

My heart started pounding again, just as it had that first day we met.

"When we began this investigation, we had to look at every angle and investigate every possibility. It's not uncommon for a nonprofit organization to be a front for money laundering. It happens far more than you'd think." He paused. "Because of that we had to look pretty closely at your organization and everyone in it."

He let that sink in.

"Of course, like I said, we found no evidence that you, your organization, or any of your employees had anything to do with the criminal activities we were investigating."

He stopped there, as if he expected that to mean something to me. He let it hang for what felt like hours.

Finally, he continued. "What I mean to say is, I think you need to watch one of your associates closely. I don't think he is the person you think he is, and I don't think he demonstrates the values of your ministry."

What he meant to say was, even though they didn't find anything related to their case or anything illegal, that didn't mean they didn't find anything at all. They found something they weren't even looking for. Something morally questionable.

Here, in our ministry?

"Yes, sir. I will look into things," I heard myself saying.

As he walked away, I thought, *Who could he possibly be talking about?*

But I didn't need to ask. Intuitively, I already knew.

They found something they weren't even looking for. Something morally questionable was going on with one of my employees.

Conducting My Own Investigation

As a child growing up in the sixties, my life centered on church, school, and our extended family. My parents lived their priorities of faith, family and friends, and then work, in that order.

We lived in a pretty protected world. Trust came easy. I am sure it happened, but I wasn't aware of people betraying other people. Perhaps my parents didn't want to destroy my innocent outlook on life, so I'd never heard of any such thing.

By the time I was a teen, I knew going into the Christian ministry was my life's vocation.

At fourteen, I announced my intentions. I immediately began speaking where I could. Church services focused on reaching "the youth of America" were popular and the norm was to have a committed high school student or young adult speak.

That is where my ministry began.

At twenty, I organized a nonprofit to fulfill my mission to make an eternal difference in the life of every person I encountered. In 1984, we organized our first camp, a successful event that drew high school students and their chaperones from all across Alabama.

Over the next ten years, we conducted more student events, and along the way we added conferences for women, men, and senior adults.

Our organization grew rapidly.

One of the people I asked to join our team was a friend I met while speaking in churches. We shared similar backgrounds and held the same convictions.

After our conferences were established, I hired him to work with us. He had a way with people that I often lacked. At the time of his hiring, most of our workers were contracted for short terms, usually to work a camp or conference. More team members followed him, of course, and we started doing regular events. Soon, we were a leader in Christian conferences, especially in the South.

Everything seemed to be going great. That is, until the day those federal agents walked into my office.

Weeks before their arrival, I noticed a personality change in my friend. He seemed to become agitated for no reason. He insisted on taking trips that I thought were unnecessary. If I pressed him for a reason, he always provided something reasonable.

I told myself that the investigation was making me imagine things that weren't there.

Then I noticed he regularly stayed late at the office. On one occasion, when I drove by the office late one night while returning from an out-of-town trip, I saw his office light shining at 2:00 a.m. When I stopped by to see if something was wrong, he explained he was behind on paperwork and time had gotten away from him.

The same had happened to me, so what could I say?

Then after the federal agent informed me that I needed to watch one of my employees closely, I decided to do some investigating of my own. The agent didn't specify anyone or where I should look or why; however, based on my friend's unusual behavior, he was the first person I examined.

I started noting his trips and asking for more details regarding their purpose. I discovered some of the destinations stated on records were not always the exact destinations where he went, but were usually someplace nearby.

So I decided to look at his phone records. They told an even darker tale.

If you're under fifty years old, you probably don't know how telephone service worked before everyone had a cell phone. Back then, every phone was a landline. That meant you couldn't easily sneak a nonwork related call to someone unless you left the building. You either had to go home or to a pay phone. Every phone was confined to one place, such as a kitchen wall or an office desk.

In addition, every phone had more than one account. You would get basic phone service from a local carrier for local calls, but to call beyond your area code, you had to contract with a long-distance provider. You negotiated a per-minute fee for every call made outside of your immediate area—generally, the farther away the other end of the call was, the higher the rate.

In order for you to verify the accuracy of your bill each month, long-distance carriers sent a list of the time, the number called, and the length of each call. If you wanted to see who someone in an office was calling and for how long, all you had to do was look at the long-distance bill, something we kept filed with our other records.

I pulled the long-distance bill for my friend's office phone and did a quick review. What jumped out were numerous calls lasting more than an hour, most of them made after our offices had closed for the evening.

Some occurred after midnight and lasted for two or three hours.

So I called a couple of the numbers and learned they were private homes. When I asked what business they had had with my employee, I either got cold silence if it was a woman or disavowal of any business at all if it was a man.

One woman hung up on me. That was highly suggestive of one thing.

So I started putting together the area codes with my friend's travels and expense reports. Times and areas often matched up. I called to check up on people he'd said he'd been flying out to meet. Most of them didn't know what I was talking about. If they did, the meetings were brief and certainly didn't require the three or four days my employee said. The majority stated they didn't have any meetings set up and never saw him.

Clearly there were some things going on that were violating the trust I had placed in him.

But innocent until proven guilty, right? He deserved the opportunity to explain himself. As the Bible says, "If your brother sins against you, go and tell him his fault, between you and him alone. If he listens to you, you have gained your brother" (Matthew 18:15). I am a man of faith who understood the importance of forgiveness, so out of a deep friendship and love for him, if something unseemly was going on, I resolved I would walk with him through repentance and recovery.

I was willing to pay what it cost, do what was necessary, and suffer the consequences. It was a decision I would live to regret more than once.

The Confrontation

Numerous organizations produce conferences and retreats around the world. Many are secular companies that train executives or teach individuals how to maximize their skills. Others just organize the logistics for companies to do their own presentations.

Within Christian circles, most major denominations have a department or individuals to coordinate and plan their events. Still others, like our organization, Phil Waldrep Ministries, conduct conferences for a cross-section of churches and individuals to attend.

Whether secular or religious, meeting planners live in a world filled with details. Forget one thing and a whole event can come crashing down.

"Joe, when will the food for the reception arrive?"

"Food? I knew there was something I forgot."

Missing a detail like that is a meeting planner's worst nightmare.

For us, we average one major event involving thousands every few weeks. One conference is being planned, others promoted, and another being produced, all at the same time. Every employee has a list of what's happening and what is their responsibility. It is essential for each employee to fulfill every assignment. Otherwise something will go wrong.

To avoid micromanaging, we empower every employee to make the decisions necessary to fulfill their responsibilities within certain parameters. These decisions often involve financial obligations and legally binding decisions for the organization. Trust is vital. We couldn't do as much as we do without it.

When someone violates that trust, it's never easy. But I've never faced anything like I faced the day I had to call my friend in and confront him about what I'd found.

After calling him in, I got straight to the point. I carefully revealed everything I knew.

Rather than denying it, he dropped his head and admitted that all of my worst suspicions were true. He even added some details that I hadn't deduced.

He said he was sorry. He asked for forgiveness. He asked what he could do to make it up. Looking back today a part of me wishes he hadn't acknowledged his actions.

Had he denied everything, we would have debated the

evidence, there would have been a further investigation, and I knew from the evidence I had already gathered that I could have fired him without issue.

As a Christian, however, I believe in second chances. I believe in forgiveness and reconciliation. I believe in redemption. So I had to practice what I preached.

I contacted a counselor who was a mutual friend of the two of us. It was someone I knew he trusted and who I trusted. He agreed to work with my friend.

He would soon be on the way to recovery and healing, and I could just forget anything had ever happened—or so I thought.

For the next few months, my friend played the model husband, the loyal friend, and the dedicated worker. He returned to being the responsible person I had befriended and hired years earlier. His personality and good spirits filled our office with warmth. The other employees humorously suggested that we all go to counseling if it made a person that happy.

For several months, everything seemed on the up and up.

Then I learned the weekly meetings with our counselor friend had ceased some months earlier. It had started as small things, and then grown into a consecutive chain of missed appointments. My friend blamed our busy schedules, a dentist appointment, a business trip, the need to pick up the car from the mechanic—never anything major but always an excuse to reschedule.

The familiar patterns of his earlier deceit seemed to be resurfacing.

Instead of losing sleep over it, I decided to confront him quickly and directly and not beat around the bush. I planned a meeting with him late one afternoon. With the other employees out of the building, we could have a private conversation that wouldn't be interrupted.

I hoped to put him back on the straight and narrow after a good heart-to-heart talk. Boy, was I in for a surprise.

I pointedly asked him if he was doing anything he shouldn't. To my surprise, he admitted he had not changed his activities. But this time when he told me, he didn't hang his head. He defended his actions.

Unlike our conversation the year before, now he intentionally and unrepentantly defied me.

I could fire him if I wanted, but I would live to regret it. If I did, he would turn every person I knew—every employee, our pastor, my counselor, and every mutual friend—against me.

I was glad there weren't any flies in the room. My jaw must've dropped to the floor. He told me I was a hypocrite.

He called me a busybody.

He said that I exaggerated what he was doing and was paranoid.

He told me he couldn't stand working for an organization as two-faced as mine.

Every accusation cut me to the quick. Not because they had merit, but because they were so unexpected and out of character.

Who was this man sitting in front of me? It was like he was a complete stranger.

Before he could say anything else, I asked him to leave. I managed to stop short of adding, "Before I do something I'll regret."

It's tough to describe the mass of overwhelming emotions I felt in that moment. Anger, certainly, but also embarrassment. Shame that I had been so duped. Shock at my own naiveté. I was dumbfounded. Enraged. I felt a deep desire to strike back at him. Despair. A violation of all I held dear.

The sudden realization that the world is not the wonderful,

magical, Mary Poppins-type place filled with basically good people felt earthshattering. The deep violation of the trust I just experienced made me suddenly question everything I thought about reality. It made me wonder if anyone else was lying to me as well.

The suspicion I had felt during the months of the investigation seemed to multiply a hundredfold. Now I wasn't just looking at parked cars with misgivings. I was looking at everyone I met.

Betrayal.

I went home in a fog of emotions and immediately went to my home study and typed out a resignation letter for him. We were going to meet first thing in the morning and I was going to offer him the opportunity to resign—or I would fire him on the spot.

I wasn't going to let him speak a word other than an agreement to my demands.

My wife and I prayed that I would have wisdom if he verbally attacked me again. I doubt if I slept two hours that night.

The next morning I was in my office before anyone arrived. He came in a short time later.

For a moment, I thought he'd had a change of heart. "What's up?" he asked as friendly as ever.

He really was asking, *What are you going to do?*

I took a deep breath and said, "I want to fire you."

Now the shock was on his face. He didn't think I would do it.

"But I love you," I continued, "and you have been a friend a long time. So I am going to give you an opportunity to resign. That way we both can say that you resigned to pursue other interests. At least on the surface, it will look like we are still friends. I think it will save both of us some embarrassment."

I slid the paper across my desk uncertain of what he would do. I made sure a pen was nearby.

He quietly read it, picked up the pen, signed it, and slid it back to me. He told me he'd get his things from his office and be gone in an hour.

"Okay," I said.

Then he left.

I leaned back in my chair. It felt like someone lifted an eighteen-wheeler loaded with a ton of steel off my chest.

Finally, it was over.

Or was it?

In that moment, I had no idea how deeply betrayal affects us. I didn't realize the costs of it emotionally, relationally, or spiritually.

In the seconds after thinking it was over, I had another thought: *I'm never going to be tricked like that again.*

That would be the first nail in a coffin I would fight for years to get out of. Betrayal is one thing; the decisions we make in its wake are quite another.

When you give someone your love and trust, you also give them the ability to wound and hurt you like no one else can. Once you've felt the pain of being betrayed, it changes you forever.

For several years after the betrayal, I carried with me the destructive power of that one betrayal.

Finally, I charted a path out of my despair.

The good news is, it shouldn't take you nearly as long to recover as it took me. There is a way to process the pain of betrayal but first, you must understand what you are feeling and why. Only then can your healing begin.

When you give someone
your love and trust, you
also give them the ability
to wound and hurt you
like no one else can.

Your Journey to Healing

Being betrayed is often a shock. The emotions we feel associated with it can be overwhelming. In processing your feelings to work towards healing, it's good to have an outlet for those feelings. You must find a way to look at things more objectively. Here are a couple of suggestions that helped me and will help you too as you begin your healing journey.

Start a journal.

Throughout my adult life I have read biographies of great people who impacted the world in a positive way. In doing so, I discovered that the most influential—more times than not—kept a journal. Their purpose wasn't to record their thoughts for history. No, they kept a journal for themselves. That is, it helped them process what was happening around them and how they felt about it.

Writing in a journal is a tremendous way to vent your emotions in a healthy way. It helps you understand what happened to you and how it's affecting you.

Write your story. Write poems, lyrics to a song, free write or draw. Write a letter you never plan to send to the person who hurt you or use your journal in any other way to pour out your hurt so that it's not bottled up inside of you anymore. Your goal is to control your emotions by expressing them instead of your emotions controlling you.

What you read earlier about my experience came almost verbatim from my journal. And what you will read in the following chapters will reflect my original thoughts and feelings as I expressed them in my journal.

When I write in my journal, I find it is like peeling an onion:

each layer reveals something deeper. Journaling can be a great way to identify and sort your feelings. It helps you get to the root of what's happening with you emotionally.

You might start by answering a few questions:

- *What is your story?* I shared my story with you. Can you write yours in the same way? Be sure to express your thoughts and feelings about the person or persons who betrayed you, the reactions of others and, yes, how you presently feel about God.

- *What are you feeling?* Make a list of the emotions you are feeling. Don't settle for just the surface emotions but dig deeper. Note when you first experienced that emotion and whether it is growing stronger or weaker.

- *Why are you feeling what you are feeling?* What do you think are the reasons you are experiencing each of these emotions?

Remember, the purpose of such exercises is to process your emotions, to get them out. It is not to rehearse them over and over or to experience the pain in a fresh way.

Once you have written these things down, start letting them go. Granted, it isn't easy and it won't happen overnight. But give yourself the right to step away from all of this for a bit. Write it out and then leave it there on the page. Don't take it with you. You deserve some time off.

And when you are writing in your journal, remember you are writing for you, not someone else. Someday you may destroy your journal. That is okay. I want you to remember your journal is a way to help you process your thoughts and emotions. That is the goal.

Talk with a counselor or pastor.

Find someone in a professional capacity that will listen as you tell your story and what you are feeling. We often need someone who knows how to deal with our emotions in a more professional context than just a friend.

Friends mean well but often they will reinforce your bad emotions. Often they are experiencing the same emotions as you on a lower level. They, too, feel betrayed because someone wounded the person they love (you). There is a place and a time for friends, but they often lack the tools to get you to the next level. You need more.

Find someone who counsels professionally, someone who has helped people sort out their emotions before and can help you do the same.

If you don't know a counselor, ask a church leader or a friend who you know went to counseling. In some cities, you can find counselors listed in phone directories. Be sure to ask for their credentials.

I know your response probably is, "I know that is what I need to do, but could you please tell me why it happened? And please tell me what is going to happen next."

Those are good, honest questions. So let's pause and dissect a betrayal, and I think we will find some of the answers to your questions.

Truth to Remember

Betrayal is very personal and affects us at a deep, emotional level. But it says more about the selfishness of the betrayer than it says about you. You goal is to prevent the betrayal and the betrayer from defining who you are. Be proactive—not reactive.

Two

····································

TRUST

Betrayal can only happen if you love.

—John le Carré

Emily came to me beside herself.

She and Mark had been married for three years and, despite a wonderful courtship, something had now come between them. Emily discovered Mark had been staying late at work or getting up in the middle of the night while she was asleep to look at porn on the internet.

At first he was repentant, but after two counseling sessions he said he wouldn't go back. "This is stupid," he said. "It's not like I had an affair or something. They're just videos and pictures! It's just how I blow off steam when you're too tired to have sex."

Emily didn't know how to respond.

Tom had a similar problem. He found out his wife, Rachel,

had gotten into a habit of having lunch with a coworker named Harold.

That was one issue he had to face, but then he discovered another one. He saw one of Rachel's friends at the local grocery and asked her, "How was that movie you and Rachel went to the other night? I'm not big on those chick flicks. Thanks for going with her."

The friend looked at him blankly. "What movie?" She hadn't even talked with Rachel in at least a month.

When Tom pressed Rachel about what her friend told him, she came clean. "Okay, okay, I went to the movie with Harold because I know you don't like those kinds of films. I just wanted to see it and I didn't want to go alone. It's not a big deal."

Tom's ears were burning. "Then why did you lie about it?"

Rachel looked at him blankly. "Because I knew if I told you I was going with Harold, you'd blow it all out of proportion just like you are doing right now. We're just friends! We work together. It was just a movie!"

Tom sensed there was more to their friendship than Rachel wanted to admit.

Mary loved numbers. She'd gone to college, obtained a degree in accounting, and got a job quickly once she graduated. Over the years, she worked her way faithfully up the leadership hierarchy and was now the team leader of a group of credit analysts. They would look at companies and determine how much credit could be extended based on a complicated number of different factors. She handled the responsibility for millions of dollars of investments. She was good at her job and crucial to her company, so crucial, in fact, that she was the first one the owner came to after the 2008 recession.

"Mary," he said, "this crash is going to be tough on everyone, but I think if we stay the course, we can make it through. I may have to make some salary reductions, but I think we can weather it with only a few job losses.

"The thing is, I need you to stay with us and help calm everyone down. A lot of companies are panicking, and I need you to help us keep our head.

"If you do, when we are back on our feet again, you're going to be the first one I promote. You see, I want you to be the vice president of our credit division. And that will happen when the time is right."

For the next ten years, things were tight, but they turned the ship around. They doubled down, worked extra hours, and lived with the lower pay knowing it would one day pay off. Mary continued working hard, even though her salary had been minimal. She wasn't sure when the owner was going to follow through on what he had promised, but it seemed it would be imminent.

One day her department got a visit from the owner. "You guys have saved us tons of money over the last few years," he told them. "I want you to know, we've turned the corner. I wanted to be the one to come to you personally and tell you we're making money now. Just stick with me a little bit longer and all you guys are going to get a raise. All of you are going to get a promotion. This next year will be our best yet!"

Everyone was excited and pleased—until about two weeks later.

It was then they got the email announcing the company had been sold to a larger conglomerate. They were going to move all of the accounting functions to the main headquarters and everyone in her department was "going to be let go."

Not long after that, Mary learned the owner had cashed out with a huge bonus from the sale. She was livid. She started looking through the numbers and realized her former boss had kept salaries low longer than needed to make the company look more profitable for the sale.

He must've been planning this all along! The crook!

Mary dropped her face into her hands. She couldn't believe she'd been so stupid.

Her boss's only comment? "I didn't know they were going to fire you all. I thought they were going to give you all those promotions—that you all were going to be moved to corporate. I'm so sorry, but it was nothing personal. It was only business."

It would be months before she could see clearly again. Mary was completely shattered and unsure of what she was going to do next.

Elizabeth, on the other hand, felt just as betrayed.

She had been the church organist for more than forty years. She'd been a wonderful servant to the church in that time but felt betrayed when the church decided to switch to a more contemporary format of drums, a keyboard, and guitars that pushed the organ out of Sunday morning services. "Times have changed," she was told. "We need to go with what will pull in a more contemporary audience."

She nodded her head at the time, but that didn't keep her from letting anyone willing to exchange a "good morning" with her know how she felt. She'd tell them about all of the late nights she had been there to play the music for Easter pageants or Christmas programs, how in over forty years as organist she had never been late to a service, and how she could play every song in the hymnal from memory.

"And now, no one even seems to care," she'd go on before the person found a way to sneak off. "Coming to church now, you'd never even know I'd ever been here."

The pastor and church leaders tried to reason with her. "Elizabeth, you were paid for all of those times—and paid well. We talked about this transition six months before we even made it. Times have just changed. We are so grateful for all your faithful years, but now it's time to let the next generation come in and play the music they feel brings them closer to God. If we ever need the organ played for anything, you will be the first person we talk to, but it's just not a popular instrument anymore. Can we all please move on?"

Elizabeth just sulked.

What Crosses the Line?

Betrayal isn't easy to define.

Marital infidelity is usually what comes to mind first when we hear the word *betrayal*. Or we think about a partner who embezzles money and runs off.

A friend gossips about a secret.

A company sells you a product that doesn't work.

Each of these feels like betrayal, but is it?

Usually a dictionary can help. When I opened my *Merriam-Webster*, this is what I found:

> **betray** verb
> 1. to lead astray; seduce
> 2. to deliver to an enemy by treachery
> 3. to fail or desert especially in a time of need
> 4. a: to reveal unintentionally, b: show, indicate, c: to disclose in violation of confidence[1]

The greater your emotional involvement and investment in the life of the person who betrays you, the greater the pain you will feel.

It appears the definition is clear. Many people, however, especially the betrayer, will try to minimize their actions by refusing to call it a betrayal. For example, they will say if they haven't had sex with someone outside the marriage then they haven't been unfaithful.

Many will say that business is a cutthroat enterprise and you just have to look out for yourself. *Caveat emptor*, after all. "Let the buyer beware."

So let me clarify what I mean by betrayal. Betrayal is a *violation of trust.*

The more we love the person that betrays us—as someone we are dating, as a spouse, as a friend, as a colleague or confidant—the more it hurts when they break our trust. The more you love or have invested in that person, the more earth-shattering their betrayal.

I like to think of it this way: the greater your emotional involvement and investment in the life of the person who betrays you, the greater the pain you will feel.

And closely associated with your pain is the effect the betrayal will have on your life. It changes everything.

Betrayals generally can be put into one of three categories.

First, some betrayals are one-on-one. It involves you and one other person.

The wife finds the bill for her husband's second credit card that has a bunch of dinner and hotel expenses on it. Now she fears being unwanted, divorced, and a single mom.

You sit in a meeting and discover your boss is getting a promotion because he took credit for your work. So much for being creative.

You learn that everyone knows something you shared with a friend in confidence.

Your investment advisor plays golf with you and your families vacationed together. Then you find out he stole your money and there is none in your account.

A parent may feel betrayed by their country that sent a son or daughter off to die in a war they feel was senseless and unnecessary.

Or, in my case, when I made that first call to one of the phone numbers my employee called late at night to hear a woman's voice on the other end. Your first thought is, "Houston, we have a problem."

Other betrayals affect you because you, along with other people in a group, were betrayed by a leader.

A pastor has an affair and violates the trust of his entire congregation.

A boss betrays his entire department or company, or a company may betray a loyal employee.

A teen with a drug problem steals from various members of the family to finance their addiction.

A husband drains the family accounts to pay off a gambling debt.

A volunteer, a coach, or a religious leader takes advantage of their access to young people to molest them.

A third type of betrayal may be one of the most difficult to face. It is when a betrayal isn't handled or discovered until years after the betrayal occurred.

A young child that was molested may have repressed the memories. They blamed themselves or thought, at the moment, it was normal. It wasn't until they received counseling for their marriage that they remember the betrayal in their childhood.

A wife finds letters her husband received from his lover when cleaning out his closet after his death.

Some betrayals are very private and get taken care of without many people knowing. Some are public and get splashed across the news or blasted across social media. The recent #metoo movement is a great example of that. The betrayal of men in power—what they did behind closed doors—was suddenly front-page news.

Others are the opposite. A cyberbully videos something personal and posts it to embarrass the person. It's become a chronic problem for many of our universities and colleges.

Betrayal could be one act or many. It could be an isolated incident or repeated over several years.

Betrayals aren't always intentional. Sometimes people just act selfishly without thinking of the consequences or who it would hurt.

Others carefully plan to deceive and harm.

There are betrayals that will permanently end a relationship and there are betrayals where the parties involved can be reconciled.

Each is unique in its details, but all have this one thing in common: *trust has been violated.* A standard of behavior—whether spoken or unspoken—has been broken.

But every betrayal causes the betrayed to ask, "Why?" And the answer is simple. People betray you because they are selfish. They put their interests and wants ahead of you. They may hope you aren't hurt but, if you are, so be it.

One thing is for certain about any deep betrayal. Nothing will be the same.

We Need to Accept that Nothing Will Be the Same

I don't want to be overdramatic, but being betrayed changes everything. History is full of moments that changed the world.

Like the moment Lee Harvey Oswald assassinated John F. Kennedy in Dallas, Texas. For the Greatest Generation, it was hearing that the Japanese had bombed Pearl Harbor. Everyone who experienced that remembers the fear as the war it started involved the whole world. For me, it was watching two jetliners crash into the World Trade Center on September 11, 2001.

Before those moments—even though they were much bigger in scale than our betrayals—the world was perceived one way. Afterwards, everyone saw and experienced the world differently.

Before a person is betrayed, they tend to see life as relatively good. They have a good job or a good team working for them. They may have the spouse they always wanted. They are living life and loving it.

"Oh, how wonderful it is to be alive!" Then they get betrayed.

It's as if the sun falls from the sky. It can feel like someone hit you in the head with a baseball bat. The world that was so wonderful before the betrayal is no longer trustworthy. Everything you believed to be true is suddenly called into question.

"If this person I trusted can deceive me, what else am I getting wrong? Where else am I being fooled? Maybe the world isn't such a wonderful place? Maybe God really isn't on my side."

And then it goes deeper. "What's wrong with me? Am I such a fool? Were they ever my friend? Did they ever really love me? Or maybe I'm just not loveable…" and on our thoughts spiral out of control.

Being betrayed makes us doubt ourselves and our worth.

Mentally, something powerful happens when you find out someone betrayed you. Every negative word spoken to you or about you begins replaying in your mind.

"Maybe I am stupid."

"I guess I am gullible."

"I'm ugly, clumsy, and dumb."

"I'll never amount to anything worthwhile."

It leaves us wondering whether or not we genuinely can connect with another person. Or whether we're worthy of being loved and respected. Or if the rest of the world is just out to use us for their own ends.

Before you were betrayed you may not have had everything figured out, but you felt like you were on the way to it. You felt that you had some value in the world.

Afterwards you realize everything you believed before—especially about that person and probably about yourself—was a sham.

Being betrayed stuns us. It stops us dead in our tracks. We wonder if it's safe to take one more step forward because we're not even sure we can trust the ground beneath our feet. "What if it too just falls away?"

The betrayal takes over our thought life. We lose sleep because we fear the nightmares. It can destroy our faith in trust and love.

Where we saw good before, now we see only uncertainty and darkness. The heat of our anger, our shame, and our desire to get even rises to feverish levels. We see everything around us not through rose-colored glasses, but through a blood-red haze of anger and hurt.

It's a state that's not only unhealthy for ourselves, but also to everyone around us. The people who still love and care about us, the people who really need us, will be affected adversely if we fail to heal properly.

There is an old expression that summarizes it well: if you don't heal what hurts you, you will bleed on people who didn't cut you.

But it's not going to go away as quickly as it came. We're going to have to live with it for a while—to let our eyes clear—before we're going to be able to move on to regain any sense of hopefulness and trust.

As a person in ministry who has listened to a lot of other people's stories, I know there are things all betrayals have in common. But how we process those can be healthy or unhealthy. It can be something that allows us to become better or it can taint everything we touch with bitterness.

Actions that Allow Healing to Occur

There are some actions that will make it better and there are some that will make it worse. Looking back, here are a few things I learned that allow healing to occur:

Admit you've been hurt.

Today I still am amazed at the number of people who refuse to admit their pain from a betrayal. They tell people they are fine. Usually, it is followed by, "It's no big deal."

Well, it is a big deal. You may think you are being strong, but you are advertising your weakness. No human can experience a deep rejection and expect people to believe that you are strong enough to handle it.

Stop denying your pain and admit it to yourself.

Give yourself permission to be angry.

As Christians, we want to do the right thing. We know the

Bible teaches us to forgive those who wronged us. But at the moment, forgiving may feel impossible. In fact, your emotions may keep you from believing that you can ever forgive the betrayer.

Maybe it would help to see what is happening to you emotionally.

Psychologists agree that betrayal is a very traumatic experience. And the closer we are to the betrayer, the more traumatic it is. In fact, it has many things in common with Post Traumatic Stress Disorder (PTSD).

Listen to these signs of PTSD and see if you are experiencing the same thing: repeated intrusive thoughts, unstable emotional regulation, alternating between feeling numb and striking out in retaliation, inability to stop searching for other evidence of possible betrayal, feeling overwhelmingly powerless and broken, or needing to regain self-worth by assigning blame. [2]

Anger, in and of itself, isn't bad. The way we express or act on our anger can be. That is why the apostle Paul wrote in Ephesians 4:26, "Be angry and do not sin; do not let the sun go down on your anger."

Anger is a normal human reaction. Allowing anger to control you is not.

And the best way to control your anger is to start by giving yourself permission to be upset.

Don't tell yourself, "I've got this."

I find almost everybody who has been through betrayal immediately tries to convince themselves, "I've got this. I can handle this. I'm telling you, I can handle this." They tell themselves things like: "I realize I'm about to have a nervous breakdown, I realize I'm crying all the time, I realize I'm lashing out at every-body, but I've got it."

The fact is, though, you don't. You need help.

You need to walk through it with someone else: a friend, a counselor, a pastor, someone. Especially if you are going to try to repair the relationship with the betrayer, you need someone out-side of yourself to walk with you—and, in most cases, with the betrayer—through it.

Especially if you want to heal from it sooner rather than later.

Stop trying to be super-Christian.

We are called to forgive, but only God can forgive and forget. Too many people try to be super-Christian and convince them-selves they can forgive and forget what happened.

We will explore this deeper in a later chapter but, for now, let me tell you that forgetting is not a requirement for forgiveness. In fact, trying to forget isn't the healthiest thing to do. God doesn't expect you to make decisions based on forgetting. If a church leader betrayed you, for example, that doesn't mean you should continue attending his church even if you forgave him.

Forgiving is not forgetting. Forgiving is releasing your right to get revenge. It is refusing to settle the score if you get a chance.

Hopefully, the day will come when the thoughts of what happened no longer cross your mind daily. But if the betrayer reenters your life and you suddenly remember what he or she did, that is normal, not unspiritual.

Forgiving doesn't mean that we can't learn from painful expe-riences and find ways to avoid them in the future.

If the relationship is to be saved, accountability is a must.

It's not uncommon (as I experienced) for the betrayer to *seem* repentant. Often they plead for forgiveness and for everyone to act as though nothing happened. That is impossible because of broken trust.

Many betrayers refuse to give up their self-serving behavior. They want to eliminate the consequences of their choices. If we let them off the hook easy, it is not uncommon for them to fall back into the same pattern of betrayal again. They must be held accountable for their actions. They must stick to the process of healing themselves and those they hurt.

During the Cold War, President Ronald Reagan entered into treaties with the Soviet Union that required monitoring the Soviet's nuclear arsenal. When questioned if he trusted the Soviets, President Reagan responded, "Trust, but verify." If trust is to be regained, verification and transparency are important.

If reconciliation is a goal, I strongly recommend that you find a qualified counselor who can be objective and honest—someone who holds the offender accountable and doesn't let you give in to their demands too quickly.

Betrayal can bring past traumas to the surface.

If you've had any trauma or abuse in your childhood, being betrayed as an adult will often bring those memories back unfiltered and virtually unconsciously. It can trigger memories as well that may have been repressed or been buried. It resurrects the raw emotion that multiplies whatever you are feeling now and will significantly complicate your healing process. There will be a need to sort out what is past from what is present, and also the need for making a conscious decision to forgive more than one person.

The ability to work through your pain today may be rooted in your ability to address a pain from your past.

We cannot let the betrayal determine our worth.

As a rule, betrayal is much more about the betrayer than it is about the betrayed. There is usually little the betrayed person or people could have done to avoid being the victim of the betrayal. Regardless, you cannot let their actions determine who you are or how much you feel loved by others. There is not an inherent flaw in you. As good people, we trust and love others—life would be empty without those. Healing will not come from shying away from trusting and loving again but in finding a way to do both in a healthier way.

At the same time, healing does not mean everything will go back to the way it was before. That is impossible. There was hurt and there was loss. While trust can be restored, it will never be the same again. While two can find love again, the traumatized partner will always be more vigilant about the other's free time and activities than they were before.

After betrayal, the world is indeed different. Something has turned it upside-down. You will never again perceive it as safe and benevolent as you once did. That can turn to bitterness or that can be turned to wisdom. The choice is up to you.

Because of betrayal, things have changed. It may be hard to grasp, but something better can come from your pain.

We have the choice in our hands: will we be part of the transformation or is the world just broken now and we need to do the best to protect ourselves so that we can survive it? Allow the Lord to heal your hurts; He can turn your pain into something good.

Your Journey to Healing

When we are betrayed, we often go into a state of emotional shock. It's hard to think. It's hard to reason, and we often just want to lash out.

Allow the Lord to heal your hurts; He can turn your pain into something good.

To help you keep life in perspective, I want you to pick up your journal and write your answers to these questions. It will help you see what *hasn't changed* in your new reality.

Count your blessings.

- What can you still count on in your life?
- Who do you know that you can still trust? (Remember, don't let the betrayal of one person keep you from seeing others in your life that you can trust.)
- What do you still enjoy?
- Who can you still count on?

Do something you love where you don't have to think about your betrayal.

As we'll discuss in a later chapter, the repercussions of experiencing a betrayal seem to color everything around you. It can take up an overwhelming amount of your thought life. Are there things you like to do that could be a distraction from those thoughts? Bowling? Golf? Bike riding? Playing pickup basketball or volleyball? Anything that is social and allows you to focus on something else will have numerous benefits.

Now that you understand what happens when betrayal occurs, I want us to examine the greatest betrayal in human history. As we do, you probably will learn a lot about the person who betrayed you.

Truth to Remember

Betrayal is a devastating blow to your trust in a person or a group of people. Your feelings and your reactions are real, raw, and natural. Admit your disbelief and anger. Start processing them in a healthy way.

Three

....

JUDAS

Jesus said to him, "Judas, would you betray the
Son of Man with a kiss?"

—LUKE 22:48

A few years ago, a lady asked to speak with me at one of the events our organization sponsors. She was a single, godly lady who was very active in her church. Since she had no children of her own, her niece and her nephew were the apples of her eye.

Her sister and her husband were involved in their church and well respected in their community. They seemed like the perfect family.

Hearing all of this, I couldn't believe the story she told me after we sat down together near the product area. The lady had such sorrow in her eyes as she relayed the details. I couldn't help but feel her pain with her.

"When she was about fourteen," the lady told me, "unbeknownst to any of us, my sister's daughter started experimenting with drugs. For a long time, the problem grew without anyone realizing it.

"Then when she was sixteen, her mom found a prescription bottle in the pocket of her jeans while doing the laundry. She didn't recognize the name on the prescription. When her mother confronted her about it, she got defensive.

"They went to counseling, but it only seemed to get worse. One night they came home and found her unconscious on the floor of her bedroom, and they couldn't wake her up. They called an ambulance and she had to have her stomach pumped. They were at their wits' end.

"So they told her she either had to go to rehab or move out. They didn't know what else to do. They told her that they loved her, but they couldn't watch her destroy herself. She'd always been such a good girl. They never imagined she would disagree.

"Instead of rehab, however, she grabbed some things and walked out."

I could see the tears gathering in the corner of her eyes, but rather than interrupting, I let her go on.

"She came to my house and asked if she could stay until she could figure things out. She said she just couldn't stand the fighting anymore. I thought she'd go home again after she cooled off. I didn't want her sleeping in the streets—she is my niece, after all—so I told her she could stay a couple days, but she'd need to work things out with her parents. I didn't know how else to help.

"The next afternoon I came home and she was just gone. I hoped she'd gone home, but she hadn't. No one knew where she went. We called the police. Her parents filed a missing person's report. She seemed to have just vanished into thin air.

"We feared the worst."

A tear started down her face.

"To make matters worse," she finally went on, "about a week later I came home and found the front door ajar and my house in a mess. Someone had broken in. They took everything. They took my jewelry and my mother's jewelry that I was saving to give, hopefully, someday to my daughters when they married. They'd taken everything of value they could find. There was broken glass everywhere.

"They even found the money I hid in my bedroom, stashed in a box in an air vent. They took my Grandma Agnes's silver. They took everything. And anything they didn't think worth taking they just threw against the floor or smashed. It was awful.

"I was devastated. On top of everything I had been through with my niece, to get robbed? It was just too much."

She looked at the ground, not knowing what to say next. Her friend who had joined us reached over and put her arm around her.

"I called the police again, of course," she continued. "I filed a report, answered all their questions, did the best to list everything that was taken. The police were there for a couple of hours. I hardly slept that night.

"The next day the police called to tell me they had found some of my stuff and knew who the robbers were. 'It was your niece and her boyfriend,' the officer told me. I couldn't believe it. He didn't say anything for what felt like a long time. Then he asked, 'Do you want to press charges?'"

This heartbroken lady grabbed her friend's forearm and looked up at me. The tears were now streaming freely down her face. "What I want to know is two things," she said. "First, what's the Christian thing to do? Should I press charges? And two, after all I've done for her, how could she do this to me?"

I have to admit, I didn't have a good answer for either question. Her story broke my heart.

Betrayed with a Kiss

It's hard to understand why betrayal happens. Many wonder what they did wrong to allow someone to betray them. But if we're going to hold victims of betrayal to be at fault, we would have to count it as the first sin Jesus committed when He allowed Judas to betray Him.

And we know Jesus didn't sin.

Think about that. Judas actually walked with Jesus on the earth for three-and-a-half years. He saw the miracles Jesus performed. He heard Jesus teach. When they escaped the crowds, Judas was one of the few who were allowed to go with Jesus behind closed doors. He heard Him privately explain what He had just taught. He was an insider.

Jesus must have even answered Judas's questions. (How many of us wouldn't love an opportunity for that!) Judas spent over three years in the presence of perfect love, and yet, on the night Jesus was arrested, Judas was the one who led the soldiers to find Him.

Judas experienced the trust of Jesus and the other disciples. They all trusted Judas completely. The Gospels tell us that of all the twelve disciples, Judas was the one they chose to be in charge of the group's funds (John 12:6). If there was giving to be done,

Judas was the one who went and did it. If there were expenses to be paid, Judas's was the only signature needed to approve the check.

Even though Matthew was a tax collector and probably very good with figures and money, Judas was the one trusted with the common purse—one that had enough money in it, in fact, that when Judas stole from it, no one else seemed the wiser. And chances are he stole from it on numerous occasions.

Judas didn't just betray Jesus but also the other eleven disciples and all who followed Jesus. Perhaps that is one of the reasons why the Gospel writers wrote so little about him—they still felt the sting of his betrayal, even decades after the event. Other than in the lists of the disciples, Judas is mentioned only about sixteen times in the four Gospels (most of those in the book of John, the last of the four to be written). And despite the fact that Judas was likely the most trusted and well-respected among them—and probably one of the most well-liked—none of these mentions have anything good to say about him.

The fact is that when the disciples asked which of them was going to betray Him, Jesus told them, "It is he to whom I will give this morsel of bread when I have dipped it" (John 13:26). Jesus then handed the morsel to Judas. Matthew tells us Judas said, "Is it I, Rabbi?" and Jesus answered, "You have said so" (Matthew 26:25).

At that point, it would seem pretty obvious who the betrayer was, wouldn't it? But the disciples still didn't suspect Judas. They suspected themselves more. When Judas left, they probably thought Jesus was sending Judas out to give something to the poor or make more arrangements for the Passover festivities.

That was how respected he was. No one ever suspected that he would betray them.

So why did Judas betray Jesus? What did he have to gain from it? Was it just for the money? Or did Judas have some darker motive?

Historical accounts suggest that Judas was a devoted Jewish nationalist. [3] He probably followed Jesus because he expected Jesus was going to instigate a rebellion to overthrow the Roman authorities. That was a common belief about the coming Messiah at that time and that's what many hoped for. They longed for a national hero to deliver them from Rome.

Few suspected that the kingdom of God Jesus came to establish would be a spiritual, not a political, one.

Some scholars suggest that Judas may have seen his betrayal as the catalyst of just such a revolution. When they arrested Jesus, Judas expected the Jews would rise up against the Romans in protest, crown Jesus as King, and fight to liberate them from Rome. They point to the fact that Jesus even seemed to be instructing Judas to go and turn Him in when He said, "What you are going to do, do quickly" (John 13:27). Some suggest that Judas believed the whole thing was sanctioned by God and his betrayal helped make God's will a reality.

The lies betrayers tell to justify their actions are usually a twisted version of the truth.

The Jewish leaders who opposed Jesus feared the people. They also feared the crowds who had just a few days before welcomed Jesus into Jerusalem as if He were a delivering king. When Judas saw the crowds were thronging Jesus, he must've thought the end of Roman rule was in sight.

A public arrest of Jesus, though, would certainly cause a scene

The lies betrayers tell
to justify their actions
are usually a twisted
version of the truth.

and perhaps start a riot. The Jewish leaders needed to find someone who knew where Jesus would be staying or where they could arrest Him in private. Judas, a member of Jesus's inner circle, was just the man they needed. When he came to them to offer his services, they were glad to pay him whatever he asked.

What went through Judas's mind that night as he made his way through the quiet streets of Jerusalem to meet the chief priests and Pharisees? Did he have any idea what would happen to Jesus after He was arrested? Probably not, since Judas panicked when he saw that Jesus was going to be condemned to death. Why did he do what he did?

We can only speculate. Those who were there with Jesus that night gave us details of nothing but his actions.

The night he betrayed Jesus, Judas was issued a band of soldiers and a couple of officers to go and find a quiet place to apprehend Jesus. It was dark. To avoid any mistaken identities, Judas told them, "The one I will kiss is the man; seize him" (Matthew 26:48). It is interesting to note that when Peter drew his sword and swung at one of the officers, cutting off his ear, it was a soldier he attacked, not Judas. Perhaps even in the midst of the betrayal they still could not fathom what Judas had done.

Then the tides turned. The Jewish leaders revealed they wanted Jesus executed. Rather than revolt, the people turned on Jesus. During Passover, it was a custom for a Jewish prisoner to be pardoned and released. Instead of Jesus, the crowd pleaded on behalf of the notorious criminal Barabbas.

Judas faltered.

There would be no uprising or revolution. Judas would not be the hero who helped spark the deliverance of Jerusalem. Instead, he was the one who helped turn Jesus over to Roman hands. Even the priests Judas had helped turned on his cause, crying, "We have no king but Caesar" (John 19:15). If Judas had any hopes of resurrecting Jewish nationalism, at that point, they were crushed.

Seeing what he had done, Judas tried to recant. He told the high priests and elders, "I have sinned by betraying innocent blood" (Matthew 27:4). They mocked him, "What is that to us? See to it yourself" (Matthew 27:4). Judas, who betrayed Jesus, now was being betrayed by the priests and elders.

In complete despair, Judas threw the thirty pieces of silver into the temple and ran into the streets. Before the morning dawned, he hanged himself having nothing left to live for. It certainly could not have been the sequence of events he had expected to happen once he walked out of the Last Supper and went to meet with the Jewish religious leaders.

The Root of Betrayal

So why did Judas betray Jesus? Why did the niece betray her aunt?

Why did my friend betray his wife, our organization, and me?

How could anyone ever do anything like that to another person?

Why does anyone ever betray anyone?

I think it boils down pretty simply, though the details are often more complicated.

Betrayal is an act of selfishness. It chooses something the betrayer wants over respect for and loyalty to another person or a group of people. In a situation that presents a trade-off between something the betrayer wants and hurting another person, the betrayer is willing to trade in that relationship to get what they want. They choose selfish gratification over love.

But, truthfully, it's not really even a choice for them. They don't see it as a trade-off. All they see is what they want. Chances are, they weren't even considering what it might do to anyone else when they did it.

And, to make matters worse, they use your trust and care for them to hide their actions. Betrayers use the other person's goodness against them. It is the very fabric of the betrayer's deceit.

Betrayers always put themselves above other people. They tend to feel their actions are completely justifiable and logical. They don't consider the pain they will cause if the other person finds out. Violating trust is just a means to an end. That doesn't mean they hate that person, it just means they don't value them as much as what they want for themselves.

For example, I think there are a lot of cases where a man has an affair, but he doesn't hate his wife. He just chooses his own selfish sexual desire above the risk of hurting his wife.

Plus betrayers tend to convince themselves they'll never get caught.

I think the niece honestly loved her aunt. At some level, she might have been grateful. But ultimately, for the betrayer, selfishness wins. There was something she wanted short term—cash for drugs, in her case—and the aunt had things she could steal to get that money.

She probably justified that her aunt didn't really need those things—she was alone and didn't have kids, after all, and most of those things she didn't use anyway. The niece had access to her house. She had a key and she knew the alarm code. The things were so easy to take. So why not take them?

The niece might have reasoned she could pay her aunt back later. Maybe she thought her aunt would forgive her as she always did, or her aunt wouldn't know it was her and her boyfriend. She made some justification to herself that drowned out the voice of reason that not only said, "This is wrong," but also, "If you do this, you are going to deeply hurt someone you love."

In the heat of the moment, I don't believe betrayers think of what they are doing to others. They think only of what's in it for them. Ultimately, selfishness drowns out both their love for others and the voice of reason and right. I think every betrayal, in its own way, is an allegiance to something other than love, other than the person they are hurting. Betrayers are willing to trade relationships for whatever it is they want.

It's a crisis of character.

When it comes right down to it, there's a broken identity in them they think they can fix by fulfilling what they want more than staying faithful to you. They are wrong, of course, but that's not how it feels to them. They feel like they need it, they have to have it, that they even deserve it. They are convinced no one will ever find them out, even though someone always does.

Most of the time they start by making small trade-offs, too small to even notice. It begins with some small betrayal that no one else notices.

The niece probably started stealing money or little things from her parents and her aunt to sell to buy drugs long before she considered breaking into her aunt's house.

Judas took money from the common purse when no one else was looking.

Slowly those betrayals grew bolder and less ambiguous. With each act their consciences grew quieter, until they were seared and silenced. There was no longer a voice in their head telling them to consider the consequences of their actions.

Betrayals start as little things and grow bigger. The person doesn't expect to get caught, but each little trade-off inches them closer to the day they will. Each small betrayal demands they justify their actions to themselves over and over again until they have no clue how ridiculous their excuses sound.

"My spouse isn't meeting my needs, so I need to find someone who will."

"You didn't stand for the things I thought you did. You're the one who changed, not me."

"Yeah, I know what I said, but that's not what I meant. You misunderstood me."

"Oh, it was only little things. You didn't really need them anyway."

"You probably would have done the same thing if the tables were turned."

It all sounds perfectly logical to them. But you know that if you were in their shoes, you wouldn't have betrayed them. That's the difference between a betrayer and those they betray. The one they betray usually never considers doing anything like what the betrayer did. They value the relationship more than what they want personally. They are glad to deny themselves those things to be closer to that person.

It's a completely different mindset, and that's what makes betrayal so inconceivable.

Before a major betrayal, the seeds of that betrayal have usually been sown again and again for years. Alone, with no one else looking, the deceiver decided to fulfill their own desires or meet their own wants over and over again.

Perhaps it has to do with meeting the craving of an addiction. Perhaps it has to do with paying off an embarrassing debt from gambling. Perhaps it makes them feel more powerful, success-ful, or desirable. No matter what it is, they trade in little bits of other people's trust to get some little thrill or meet a small desire for themselves.

Over time that builds towards some moment that is almost equal to temporary insanity. The only explanation the other dis-ciples ever gave for what Judas did was that "Satan entered into him" (John 13:27). "Judas would never have done such a thing on his own," they might have reasoned. "He couldn't have been in his right mind. The devil must've made him do it." In fact, this is exactly what happens. Evil gains a stronger and stronger hold until evil rules the heart.

It probably took them some time to unravel all the little deceptions that led up to singling Jesus out for those soldiers. Somehow Judas always came down on the side of money in a way that made it sound charitable, but he was just looking for ways to cover his thefts.

When the woman poured expensive perfume on Jesus's feet and wiped them with her hair, Judas was the one who asked, "Why was this ointment not sold for three hundred denarii and given to the poor?" (John 12:5). It wasn't until afterwards that the disciples realized he asked that so there would be more money in their funds after he'd spent some of it on himself.

You don't really notice all the little signs of betrayal until after the fact. While those of us who are betrayed always assume we should have figured things out earlier, the truth is we didn't because we didn't see them. And even if we had, chances are we would have shrugged them off as something else. Someone else either has to point them out or we don't see them until later.

That is why, looking back, you feel stupid. You start asking yourself, "How could I have missed the obvious?" The reason is it wasn't obvious because you loved that person and had grace for them.

The betrayer is a friend, a loved one, someone we have known for years, if not most of our lives. They are someone we trust and, therefore, we always give them the benefit of the doubt when there are small discrepancies or indiscretions. They are someone we love, which is a big part of why betrayal hurts so much.

And there is another part of the problem. Betrayers don't tend to be the underhanded, sniveling deceivers we sometimes see in movies where everyone except the person who is under their spell sees what the person is up to. Betrayers are charismatic, friendly, and can even appear altruistic, generous, and loving. They play the part of being a good, moral person who is above reproach so that nothing interferes with their secret life.

Remember Bernie Madoff, who admitted to running one of the largest Ponzi schemes in history? People said he was one of the nicest men they had met. As a result, people trusted him with all their money.

Or Dennis Rader, the famous BTK strangler who murdered at least ten people in Wichita, Kansas? No one suspected him because he was the president of his local church council and a Cub Scout leader.

Betrayers are victims of their own desires. They often have troubled pasts or have fallen prey to an addiction. It's safe to say that if a person had no such issues and they were given the trade-off between a selfish desire and staying in relationship with a loved one, they would choose to preserve the relationship. That is what I would do, and I would guess that is what you would do too.

Betrayers, however, have worked their way—one small justification at a time—into making the opposite choice. It doesn't excuse their actions in any way, but it does leave the door open to compassion. It does leave the door open—if they are truly repentant—for them to be restored.

It's just that we need to be very careful about how we go about that.

Could Judas Have Been Forgiven?

It's hard to look at the story of Judas and not wonder if he was forgivable after his fall into betrayal. Obviously, in the end, he appeared sorry for what he had done.

When the hopes he had in betraying Jesus didn't materialize, and when he saw the harm he had done and how he had helped condemn Jesus, I think it is possible that he would have undone it all if he'd had the chance. But we simply don't know.

Judas was short-sighted. He didn't know what we know today. He didn't know what was on the other side of the cross.

In some ways it seems as though Judas didn't hear a word Jesus said about the forgiveness of sins or salvation in the three and a half years he walked with Him.

When the "kingdom" Judas was expecting didn't manifest after Jesus was arrested, all he saw was despair. All he saw was Jesus's blood on his hands. He didn't foresee a resurrection. He didn't comprehend the spiritual kingdom Jesus had come to establish. He didn't see what the sacrifice of Jesus would accomplish. All he saw was a future he couldn't bear to face. So he exited out of it by hanging himself.

Had Judas not hanged himself, however—had he been able to deliver himself out of the pit of despair of that night and make it to the next dawn and then perhaps still been alive on the Sunday of Jesus's resurrection—would things have been different?

Possibly.

Had he asked for forgiveness, I believe Jesus would have extended it. Jesus died for the sin of humanity on the cross and that included Judas.

Nor was Judas really the one to carry the full weight of Jesus's crucifixion. It was the sin of all humanity that sent Jesus to the cross, not Judas's betrayal. In His perfect love and out of His sacrifice for all, Jesus would most certainly have forgiven Judas for what he did that night with a simple kiss on the cheek.

But I think the situation also begs another question: Would Jesus have let Judas back into His inner circle of trust again? Or, for that matter, would the other eleven ever have trusted Judas to be among them once more?

That is impossible to say, but I think probably not. It would depend on the sincerity of Judas's repentance and the change in his heart going forward. Only God can know a human being's heart, so only He would know whether Judas would ever be trustworthy again. Only God knows if Judas would have continued in his selfish ways. Would Judas come to understand the true purpose of Jesus coming to the earth and be able to let go of the political deliverance he had hoped for and instead preach the spiritual one Jesus made available?

It's really too much to know.

Though Jesus would certainly have forgiven Judas, I'm not so sure Judas would have become a church father unless all of the above proved true. If Judas's motives for following Jesus in the first place did not undergo a radical transformation, then there wouldn't be anything for him to build true faith upon.

The betrayer—the traitor—has a worldview that just doesn't

mesh with the world around them, otherwise they would have seen their betrayal as unthinkable as the rest of us do.

It wouldn't just be a matter of being forgiven by those they offended, it would demand a fundamental change in the way they saw the world and what they valued. They would have to forsake the selfish mindset they used to justify what they did. That would require a much deeper heart change, and one that will take time, often lots of time, to verify.

Yes, God forgives and forgets, but He also knows how to read the true intents and nature of a person's heart. We don't. It's one thing to forgive, but it's quite another to put ourselves or other loved ones in a place to be hurt so deeply—or even injured—by a betrayer again.

From my experience and my knowledge of Scripture, I don't believe we should. While we certainly don't want to keep condemning a person for a past mistake, we also don't want to give them free rein to stay in the behavior that led to the betrayal in the first place. I certainly wish I hadn't with my friend.

Perhaps if I'd had better checks and balances in place, we could have helped him more when he seemed willing.

Forgiveness can be granted freely, but trust must be earned.

We need to be smarter moving forward. We need to establish proper boundaries. But those are issues for tomorrow, not today. The first thing we must do is deal with the initial shock, the deep pain from the hurt of betrayal, and we must allow ourselves to answer the questions that come naturally.

For those of us who are fresh from a betrayal, the thought of forgiveness is often still far away. We're still reeling from the punch in the face. It still hurts so much it's hard for us to think clearly.

For those of us who are fresh from a betrayal, the thought of forgiveness is often still far away. We're still reeling from the punch in the face.

There is still more to think through. There is still more to understand about what happened. There are still more questions to be answered, not the least of which is, "Why did this happen to me?"

Your Journey to Healing

It often helps to know we're not alone and we're not the only one who has ever faced what we are facing. The Bible, as an example, is full of betrayal, starting with Cain betraying Abel (Genesis 4:1-16) all the way to Ananias and Saphira lying to the early church (Acts 5:1-11).

As you continue your journey of healing, take a moment to do the following:

Read the Psalms.

Many of us think of the Old Testament Book of Psalms as a hymnal. But it is more than songs that were sung by the Jewish people. In many ways, it is a journal where people, especially King David, recorded their feelings about the things happening to them. Their thoughts reflect a transparency and an honesty that will encourage you as you read them.

Prayerfully read what they wrote. Then take your journal and write your own psalm where you tell God exactly how you feel. Don't worry about what you write. You aren't going to tell Him anything He doesn't know already, nor is your honesty going to hurt His feelings.

(See the appendix in the back for some good psalms to start with.)

Read how Paul handled his betrayals.

Romans 8:28 tells us, "We know that for those who love God

all things work together for good." Paul also wrote that he experienced "danger from false brothers" (2 Corinthians 11:26)—in other words, betrayals. Take a look at what Paul endured in 2 Corinthians 11–12. How did he handle these things? How would you?

One thing I discovered shortly after I experienced a deep betrayal is that you evaluate every aspect of your relationship with the betrayer. You easily make a list of the ways they hurt you.

You relive every moment wondering what went wrong. Then something begins to happen. You start examining yourself. You start expressing regrets and guilt. Before long, you are asking, "What did I do wrong?"

That is perfectly normal—and that is why we are going to explore that question next.

Truth to Remember

Betrayers don't just betray you—they betray themselves. Their priorities are out of whack and they make selfish decisions as a result. You're not alone in being betrayed. Even Jesus experienced it and was able to forgive.

Four

SHOCK

There are some things in life over which God simply writes,
"I'll explain later."

—Corrie ten Boom

t's pretty common for people to feel like they did something wrong when someone betrays them. They get angry with others (and God) for not helping to prevent the betrayal. This especially is true when they find out other people knew what was happening but didn't tell them. Those emotions are very real, and they are very raw. So raw, in fact, that they can be hard to place in context.

When people come to me and ask, "What did I do wrong? What did I do to deserve this?" I ask them to imagine what it was like for Uriah to walk into paradise. Uriah, you may recall, was the husband of Bathsheba. She was the married woman that committed adultery with King David.

As far as we can tell from what is written in the Bible, Uriah had one fault: he had a beautiful wife.

One spring while his armies were off at war (Uriah is in the Israeli army), King David stayed home in his palace. Restless one balmy evening, he goes to the roof to get some fresh air.

It's late, and thinking no one else would be out, Uriah's wife, Bathsheba, goes up on the roof and takes a bath to cool off.

David happens to catch a glimpse of her, and then can't take his eyes away. The woman is beautiful. He must meet her.

So David sends for her and invites her to dinner. Not knowing what to expect, Bathsheba obeys her king's request, and David seduces her. (Not David's best moment, to be sure.) Then he sends Bathsheba on her way.

That might have been the end of things, except Bathsheba becomes pregnant. David decides to try to cover things up, so he requests Uriah be sent from the front back to Jerusalem to give him a report on the fighting.

After Uriah reported on how things were on the battlefield, David commended him. "Take a load off," he told him. "Go home, take a shower, enjoy a night at home." David, of course, expected Uriah to act as he would. If he were home for a night and slept with his wife, then everyone would expect that the child was Uriah's.

However, Uriah couldn't fathom getting a night at home when his buddies were sleeping with rocks as pillows on the front lines. Rather than going home, he slept with the servants near the palace door.

The next day David was shocked to hear that Uriah had never gone home. He called for him.

"Haven't you come on a long journey? Why didn't you go to your house to rest? To sleep on a nice bed and refresh yourself for your return?"

I imagine there was some conviction in Uriah's voice as he answered, "The ark of the covenant and the soldiers of Israel and Judah are still sleeping in tents, camping near the open battlefield. How could I go home, eat, and sleep with my wife as if we were at peace? As the king lives, I will not do such a thing."

David decided to try to wear him down. He asked Uriah to stay a few more days, and when he still didn't go home, David invited him to dinner and tried to get him drunk. Even though Uriah was more than tipsy when he left, he still didn't go to his wife.

When the report came that Uriah again slept in the servant's quarters, David wrote an order to his general, Joab, one that he would send back with Uriah. "Set Uriah in the forefront of the greatest fighting," he wrote, "and then order the rest of the troops to draw back from him that he may be struck down and die."

Joab did as he was ordered and sent Uriah against the fiercest enemy warriors, forcing them within striking range of the archers on the city walls. Several faithful soldiers died with Uriah that day in a fight Joab would otherwise have avoided.

When he sent word to David, who he knew would be angry at the foolishness of this particular attack and the loss of men, he told the messenger, "If you see the king's anger rise, then add to your report, 'And your servant Uriah the Hittite is also dead.'"

The messenger did as he was told. He delivered the message

of the defeat just as he'd been instructed. When he saw David's anger starting to rise, he said what he was told to say. Rather than a rebuke about the foolish loss of life, though, David simply said, "Tell Joab, 'Do not let this matter displease you. The sword is fickle, and losses are to be expected. Strengthen your attack against the city and overthrow it.' Tell him to be encouraged."

Then, once Bathsheba had spent a respectable amount of time mourning her husband, David made the grand gesture of marrying his fallen soldier's wife so he could care for her.

The appearance was that all was well in the kingdom.

So imagine what it was like for Uriah to meet Abraham and Moses at the gates of paradise the day of his death. He'd been a good soldier, a loyal citizen, and a faithful husband. From what we're told of him, he had been a godly man.

All the same, he was betrayed by both his wife and his king.

I can just hear him walking up to the two fathers of his faith and asking, "What did I do to deserve this? Why is it David can steal my wife and have me killed and he gets off scot-free? He's still on the throne, he has Bathsheba, and now he has what should have been my child! History will remember him as the greatest king of Israel, and I'll be just a footnote. He's on the throne and I'm in the grave! How is that fair? Where's the justice?"

I have to tell you, I feel his pain.

When Betrayers Seem to Win

Those who have read the story of David know that wasn't the end of the matter for him. The child he had with Bathsheba died, and years later David faced rebellion at the hands of his own son because of his actions, as well as other repercussions. But it was certainly the end of the matter for Uriah. There was no coming back for him. No matter what David suffered later on, Uriah was dead, and he wasn't going to get his wife back or even be allowed to move on and start a new family. His story was over.

That certainly doesn't seem fair.

And I've seen such things happen in more than just the life of King David. I've seen it happen with people I knew well.

Not long ago I spoke in a series of services at a church that had a wonderful, gifted musician as their choir leader. His wife also was involved in the music ministry. They seemed a beautiful young couple with two great kids and a great future together.

A few months after I was there, the pastor caught the music minister and the church secretary (they were the only three church employees) together in a back room. As the pastor put it, "They were neither clothed nor in their right minds." (It's funny how when people are caught like that they say, "It's not what it looks like!" What else could it possibly be?)

The pastor suspected something was going on, so he laid a little trap for them. One morning he made them think that he would be out of town for the rest of the day. Sure enough, when he returned a brief time later, his suspicions were confirmed.

Of course, the music minister and the secretary were both fired. Appalled, the music minister's wife asked for a divorce. The church was devastated. It would take them years to recover from the betrayal.

The musician and the secretary left in disgrace. If the story had ended there, perhaps it would have seemed fair. But it didn't.

The musician and the secretary ended up getting married. Eighteen months later, the pastor learned the musician had been hired as the music director at a large church in a major city in a nearby state. Calling the pastor of that church, he asked if he didn't know about their past and what they had done to his church and the man's family.

"Brother," the pastor answered, "we believe in forgiveness. Yes, they told me what happened, and our church board believes their repentance is sincere. God has forgiven them and so have we."

The man and his new wife were enjoying a big salary and living in a nice, new home provided by the church, while his ex-wife was trying to support their two children on the measly alimony payments the guy was making that were based on the fact that he had no job at the time of the divorce.

He was driving a Corvette he received as a gift from one of the members of the new church. At the same time, his innocent ex-wife and two kids were living in a rundown, 750-square-foot house. She got the only job she could at a local big-box store stacking shelves to make ends meet.

Can you imagine that she might be a little angry? Angry at God? Angry at church? When I met with her, she told me, "Forgiveness is easy when you've got talent." And, yes, her ex-husband was a very talented guy, and in a lot of situations, talent trumps character. (Just look at the controversies caused by certain players in professional sports.)

Pretty far from Judas's story of despairing and going out and hanging himself, don't you think?

How can you rectify things like that?

What would you have said to that young woman?

No Easy Answers

One of the challenges of life is that it's complicated. We live in a battlefield of contradicting information, mystifying actions by people with mixed motives, and having to live with inequities

Being betrayed hurts. And just because a Band-Aid is good to stop the bleeding, that doesn't mean the pain will go away when you put it on. Healing will take some time.

and pain we did nothing to cause or deserve. Though we may give our lives to God individually, we are still in an enemy playground where our rules for fairness don't always apply like we think they should.

It would be nice to be able to speak a few words and for everything to instantly get better.

Bless our darling hearts and our stupid heads, many of us try. We might tell people things like,

"It will work out in the end."

"You just need to forgive him (her)."

"They'll get what they are due."

"You shouldn't let the sun go down on your anger. You need to let this go."

Yes, in their context, these things are true and even scriptural. But they can be of little help in the midst of an anger so intense it's hard to see straight. Being betrayed hurts. And just because a Band-Aid is good to stop the bleeding, that doesn't mean the pain will go away when you put it on. Healing will take some time.

Most people who have been betrayed tend to run through a list of questions that goes something like this:

- How could you?
- What did I do wrong?
- Why me?
- How could I have been so stupid?
- Why didn't I see this coming?
- Why didn't somebody tell me?
- How could God have let this happen?
- If I could get away with murder, where would I hide their body?

Okay, I'm half joking about that last one, but when I talk with people in the early pain of a betrayal, the desire to get even is very real. They have a deep sense of justice that tells them things would be better if that person felt the pain they had caused. "If they would just suffer like I'm suffering now, at least things would seem fair, and maybe they would be better."

Such pain and anger won't go away just because you wish it. It needs to be processed. It needs to be addressed. It needs to be worked through.

And that will take some time.

But as you are working through your pain, remember that it's not really about what you did. Yes, you trusted them. Yes, you loved them. Yes, you gave up a lot for that person. But that's all part of a healthy relationship. The unhealthy part is not you but what they did by betraying you. Because they pursued what they wanted without considering its effect on you, the fault lies with them, not you.

Because, more often than not, you were not a factor in their thinking. David was not thinking about Uriah when he saw Bathsheba on that rooftop taking a bath. He wasn't thinking, "That Uriah—what can I do to hurt him?" He may not even have known who Uriah was at the time.

No. What he was thinking was, "Wow! Look at that woman! I want her. And why can't I have her? I'm the king. I can have whatever I want! I've done good things for my kingdom. I deserve to have whatever I want."

What did Uriah do wrong? *Nothing.*

What did the first wife of the music minister do wrong? *Nothing.* What did I do wrong with my friend? *Nothing.*

What happened simply isn't fair.

And it is often that unfairness that causes the most pain.

One thing I know is true is that you cannot correlate material or perceived blessings with the approval of God. Nor can you associate lack of blessings with the disapproval of God. The Bible tells us, "He [God] makes his sun rise on the evil and on the good, and sends rain on the just and on the unjust" (Matthew 5:45).

An instantaneous snapshot of the way things are doesn't determine the way they will end up. Appearances can be deceiving. What looks like a prosperous, happy household isn't always the way it appears. And just because things don't look sunny for you right now doesn't mean tomorrow (or a year from now) will be the same.

The thing is, you can't be responsible for how God deals with the other person—with the person who betrayed you—you have influence only over how open you are to His dealing with you.

Don't Fall into the Shame Trap

Identity is a funny thing. It's not something we think about often, but it drives most of what we do. We all want to matter in the world. We all want to be loved and respected, even if it is only for some small thing. The drive to be president of the United States has a lot in common with wanting to be recognized as employee of the month. Only the scale of the stage is different.

That sense of wanting to be significant in the universe, of being unique and special, of making a difference for others, of getting attention or being popular, is a big part of what makes us who we are. But it is also very fragile if we build it on the wrong things. Who we are in the eyes of the people who are important to us gives us a strong sense of who we are and how valid we are as human beings.

When one of those relationships is suddenly shattered by betrayal, too often we feel as though who we are is shattered as well. We become ashamed, as if the betrayal now determines who we are.

Shame is a powerful emotion. So powerful that our unconscious minds will do almost anything to protect us from experiencing it. That can lead to falling into the shame trap of denial and isolation, as if those will protect us. Instead they have a way of delaying our healing.

Denial and isolation, however, are very real and need to be acknowledged. They are the first stage of grieving for the world we lost—the world of innocence that we knew before our life was shaken to its foundations by betrayal.

In a very real sense, we have to rebuild our hope, our optimism, and our ability to trust again.

Just as 9/11 shattered our place in the world as Americans, betrayal shatters our place in the world as an individual. Our place will not be the same as it was before, but it can be restored. Believe it or not, our place can be stronger than it was before the betrayal occurred.

For that to happen, we must process the grief of our loss; we must confront our denials and avoid letting ourselves become isolated. It won't happen all at once. And it won't happen in a perfect, straight line.

Give yourself time. Give yourself an opportunity to process your emotions. Don't be hard on yourself when the anger overwhelms you again or you fall into bouts of depression. That's perfectly natural and part of the healing process. But don't grovel either. Express and process your negative emotions and give them to God. He will know what to do with them.

We must process the grief of our loss; we must confront our denials and avoid letting ourselves become isolated. It won't happen all at once.

Don't let those things have the final say in determining who you are and how you will live your life. Don't let shame win. Being betrayed doesn't have to be your defining moment. You can still live for something better. God still has great things planned for your life. Don't let betrayal derail them.

Your Journey to Healing

While the emotions of betrayal will make you want to hole up and hide, find excuses not to isolate yourself. Give yourself some "me time," but make sure some of it is out in the world that still functions and is moving forward.

Here are a few suggestions of things you might try—though don't limit yourself to these. There's a good chance you'll have ideas for things that better fit you.

Develop a new routine.

Think about what you really want out of life and create a schedule and objectives that will work to accomplish those things. It could be anything from writing a book to eating healthier. Setting new goals for yourself, working on accomplishing them, and rewarding yourself for little successes on the way can give you something healthy to focus on away from your pain.

Spend more time with your friends.

If your life requires you to interact with your betrayer (your ex-husband gets the kids for the weekend, you still see your boss because you can't find another job), find a friend or coworker who can be with you to support you. Sometimes you will need to immediately talk about your feelings because these encounters bring back painful memories. Treat these times like a professional, not a child. Make your exchanges quick and as rare as possible.

Make sure you are part of a healthy church.

If a church is healthy, it can help you process the seismic shift in relationships that's happened because of your betrayal. It gives you a place to belong and stay plugged in. It gives you a family that cares about you and a place to safely rebuild your trust of others. A healthy church will help you grow personally and walk through the toughest of times.

Get out and get some exercise.

Taking part in a dance, fitness, or stretching class, jogging, walking, even taking up boxing or a martial art all help alleviate stress and give our emotions a focus outside of ourselves. While this might not help you sort out what you are feeling as well as, say, talking with a counselor, the time spent sweating and moving will give you time away from your thoughts so you can deal with them better later on.

Remember the old saying, "An idle mind is the devil's workshop." There is an element of truth in that statement. Avoiding people, staying away from church, and withdrawing from people allow your mind to focus on the actions that hurt you. And it isn't healthy nor does it help you heal.

These are just a few of the things I've seen that help people be honest with themselves about the pain of their betrayal. Why don't you take out your journal and start writing so you can begin to put life in perspective? Take time to think about the activities I suggested above.

Does reading this list inspire some other activity?

What are you going to try to help you process the emotions you are feeling in reaction to what happened to you?

What do you need to do to start that activity sometime in the next three days? Write your responses and make a schedule. And stick to it!

By now, you probably know there is one thing that is easy for you to do. It is thinking about your pain and what the betrayer did most, if not all, the time. It is easy to obsess about your pain. But constantly thinking about your betrayal increases your pain. It doesn't lessen it.

And it has the potential to destroy the healthy relationships you still have. That is why we need to talk about it in the next chapter.

Truth to Remember

Wishing for your betrayer to feel the pain you feel only increases your pain. Stop watching for the good things that are happening to them. Focus on your recovery, not the blessings you think they are enjoying. It doesn't matter what happens to them. Leave that to God.

Five

....

PAIN

Pain changes people. It makes them trust less,
overthink more, and shut people out.

—Anonymous

A few years back, after a session at one of our conferences, a woman approached me and told me she was struggling with forgiving her husband for an affair he had, even though she "knew it wasn't his fault."

I was a bit perplexed by the statement. "What do you mean?" I asked.

"Oh, I mean, I know he loves me, and he would never do anything like that, but there was this woman at work." She paused, and then I realized she meant that as an answer.

"What do you mean?" I heard myself asking again.

"Well—I mean, he would never—but sometimes there are

needy women who go to work looking for a relationship, and it's like they don't even recognize the man is married. They just put themselves out there and they fall for their boss or someone who is kind to them in the office. The hussies! They go after the good ones. The next thing you know, they're seducing one of them."

I'm pretty sure my face betrayed my continued confusion, but I just gave her an affirmative "Uh-huh."

"Anyway, I've forgiven him," she went on, "but why can't I get over the feeling, you know? I mean, it was so much easier last time."

I felt my eyes widen. "What do you mean?"

"I mean, the last time a woman pulled him into an affair like that, I was able to forgive him and get over it—I mean, my husband's a good man—it's just that he's working in these bad places, and because he's good looking and he's a sweet man, all these women are after him. It's not his fault!" She took a big breath. "But this time, even though I've forgiven him, I just can't seem to get over the feeling."

I shook my head slightly, as if something was wrong with my ears. "What feeling?"

"The feeling that I want to claw the woman's eyes out!"

Again she paused, but this time I couldn't make a sound. I was at a complete loss.

"Well?" she finally went on. "What do you think I should do?"

I just stared into her imploring face as she waited for "the man of God" to give her some profound answer. But I had nothing. I was dumbfounded.

"I think," I finally managed, "I think you...I think you should take some time to talk with one of our workers."

She nodded, and I called someone over to take her to speak

with someone who I knew would help her get more professional help than we could provide.

When the Pain Is Just Too Much

It would be easy to dismiss a case like this as one of a kind. I wish it were. While this woman's situation might be a little extreme, I see people react to the pain of betrayal in similar ways all the time. In the same way that denial is the first part of the grieving process, I believe the painful emotions of betrayal send us through a similar cycle.

I know that might sound a little strange. I mean, after all, no one died. What loss would the person be grieving?

I believe it is the loss of the relationship. It is the stinging realization that your trust and devotion meant so little to them. There is the death of a friendship, the death of a partnership, the death of a family or business, the death of a marriage. And because there's been a death, a loss, we find ourselves reeling from emotions. And we don't know how to deal with them or handle them.

If we have a loved one die from cancer or in a car accident, there's a reasonable object for our hurt, anger, and sorrow. Part of the process is bargaining with ourselves about what we might have done differently—perhaps if we had helped them eat better or if we hadn't sent them on an errand for us, our loved one would still be alive today. All of that is natural. It is expected that people hate cancer or lament the dangers of driving. No one did anything intentionally to cause the death.

Betrayal is different.

The person we trusted had absolute control over whether they betrayed us or not. That makes the bargaining all that much more poignant. It's not just the betrayal but that we were gullible enough to allow them to betray us. By acknowledging what they did, we implicate ourselves as well. If they're guilty, so are we. They may have been devious, but we were fooled by them. Which is worse?

So to deal with the pain, we deny what happened. We displace the responsibility. We project the blame. We want to pretend it never occurred.

Or we try to bury it. We put on our super-Christian T-shirt and plead forgiveness, and then feel even more guilty when that doesn't make the pain go away. We pretend we can handle it. That it doesn't faze us. That we can move on as if nothing happened.

How do I know? Because that's what I did.

Don't Set Up Residence in the State of Denial

In the three years following my friend's second betrayal, I did nothing to deal with it. I did nothing to process the emotions I felt because of it. I just went on as though nothing had happened. I continued going to churches. I continued speaking. I continued building our organization and trying to minister to people.

Though I don't recall making a conscious decision about it, I had decided to do the big boy thing—I was going to forgive and forget. I was over it. I wasn't going to let it affect me.

As if that were possible.

What I did instead was internalize the anger I felt against my friend. And with it the shame at being fooled by him. But you can't bury emotions like that. They'll still come out. But they will come out looking like something else.

As I shared before, I grew up in a functional family surrounded by a supportive network of relatives and friends. We had a wonderful church community. I had a great mom and

I had decided to do the big boy thing—I was going to forgive and forget. I was over it. I wasn't going to let it affect me. As if that were possible.

dad, and my mother grew up in the church we attended, so everyone knew who I was. My mother was one of eleven children—nine of whom lived to adulthood—and all her brothers and sisters went to that same church. It felt like I was related to half the congregation. (I was an only child, so I sometimes joke I got the love my mom had for all her brothers and sisters dumped on me.)

My father's family lived nearby and also shared the same values. So I grew up in a world full of people I could trust without reservation. It was very innocent and protected—it fit the classic myth of the small American town. Everyone knew each other and watched out for each other. It was everything short of having a barn raising every month.

After my friend's betrayal, that began to slowly change. I began questioning things. Who else was out there, like him, fooling other church people? If they were all being fooled, how did I know I could trust what they said or did? How could I trust their judgment in other matters?

How could I trust them about anything?

In the matter of three years I went from trusting everyone and thinking the world was a positive and happy place to trusting no one and seeing mostly darkness and hopelessness.

It is hard to minister to other people from that pessimistic viewpoint.

And it takes its toll on your soul as well. When your inside world doesn't line up with your outward disposition, the hypocrisy is like a rot. Subconsciously, you try to rectify the two. I started trying to justify my friend's actions. Maybe there really was something wrong with his marriage. Maybe something had happened to him as a kid and he never told anyone. Maybe he had some kind of addiction. Maybe he wasn't completely in control of his actions.

But there comes a point when you're standing in a downpour in the middle of a thunderstorm and you are forced to finally come to the conclusion it's raining. Things that only irritated me before began to make me angry. And things that used to make me angry now made me really, really mad.

Things were out of proportion.

Of course, it wasn't the situations that were at fault, it was anger at my friend—an anger I had never expressed that was finding a way to piggyback on every little thing that bothered me. I blew things out of proportion.

You would never have known. It wasn't like I would unleash my anger on others. Looking back, that may have been even healthier than what I did do. I just pushed things deeper. I would smile on the outside and rage on the inside.

Then I'd be ashamed of the anger.

It was a horrible cycle.

And rather than letting anyone else know what was happening with me, I just withdrew further into isolation.

Somewhere in there I realized that my life was good, my marriage was good, and my family was wonderful. But life had no taste. I had no joy. Something was sucking the oxygen out of the air I breathed.

I needed to do something.

It's hard enough as a normal person to start seeing a counselor, but can you imagine how it is for a preacher? I knew I needed help, but I didn't want the stigma of asking for it. That is when I compromised. A friend of mine who is a counselor agreed to meet me for a session or two outside of his office. We would meet in a coffee shop or over lunch. It would look just like two friends having lunch, but I was there because I needed someone to help me figure things out.

You know what he told me?

He told me I needed to face my repressed emotions and deal with them. I needed to confront them head on and process what I was feeling.

It was one of the hardest things I've ever done. But it's also been one of the most freeing.

I needed to acknowledge that I'd been hurt and how much I'd been hurt. I needed to allow myself to "be angry and...not sin" (Ephesians 4:26). I needed to process my emotions, and the first step of that was to acknowledge I had them.

We ended up meeting together like that for several weeks.

Facing the Pain of Betrayal

You can't deny emotional pain away. A growing number of experts recognize that our bodies remember trauma that we've faced (even when we don't). And if we don't deal with the emotions connected to that trauma, the pain can manifest itself in different ways—usually as some other physical pain or injury.

Right now in the United States, there is a record number of cases of chronic pain that prompts people see their doctor. No matter what is prescribed, the pain doesn't go away. But then some of those same people go to therapy and are confronted with the connection of their pain with the trauma of their past, and then they never experience the pain again. Granted, most physical pain has a physical cause. Everyone experiencing physical pain should first see a physician. But if the pain does not go away, dealing with trauma can often help.

We often wonder why the pain won't go away, and why it seems to reverberate to every other relationship we have, like the waves from a rock thrown into a lake. It is due to the fact that we haven't confronted our pain and dealt with it in a healthy way.

And the greater that pain, the more we need to do it.

The pain of betrayal is relative. It depends on the kind of relationship we have with the person. It depends on how long we've known them. And it depends on the degree of the betrayal.

After thinking about it for years, I came up with a little formula that helps me understand the pain caused by a betrayal. I think of it this way:

The pain of betrayal equals the level of trust times the amount of investment.

Let me illustrate. Suppose a young person came to my door and told me they were having a subscription drive to raise money for their school. I give ten bucks for a subscription. And the magazine never comes. I might be upset. Odds are I would not do anything or say anything about it. At the most, I might call the school and say something. But after I dealt with it, that would be it. I lost ten dollars but there wasn't any residual, lingering pain. It was a small degree of trust in someone I'd never met. I experienced very little pain, if any, because I had only a small investment of time and money.

I'd get over that pretty quickly.

But let's say an investment advisor talked me into investing twenty thousand dollars in a company. I later find out that he knew it was a failing company and only wanted to help a family member get rid of some bad stock. Since I lost more (in this case, part of my hard-earned savings), my anger and pain would be greater than losing just ten dollars in a subscription drive. The higher level of investment is going to mean the betrayal hurts more. Especially if there's no way to recover the investment.

That pain will mask a lot of other feelings as well: humiliation, anger, vulnerability, self-confidence, self-respect, sorrow, horror, depression, regret, abandonment, rejection, frustration, loneliness, fear, hatred, bitterness, and so many others.

It can damage the way we see the world and the people in it. It can suck hope out of the air we breathe.

Such things don't go away without being confronted.

We need to address the pain and work through it. Then we need to address each of the underlying emotions. We need to confront the lies that a betrayal makes us a lesser person or unlovable. We need to get back to seeing the world for the miraculous place it is and not see more potential betrayal around every corner.

We need to have our faith in love and trust restored again.

The Death of Trust

Recovering from betrayal is a grief process.

Often people try to minimize a betrayal by telling someone who has been betrayed, "It's not like anyone's died." But I disagree. Yes there has been a casualty; at the very least, it is your trust. And, often, there is the death of a relationship, partnership, or a friendship. There may even be the loss of a business, a reputation, or a life savings.

According to psychologists, the top three most stressful or traumatic life events are (1) the death of a spouse, (2) divorce, and (3) marital separation.[4] Further down the list is the death or sudden loss of a close friend. (It's worth noting that "being betrayed" was not considered when creating this list, or it might well be near the top.)

Regardless, in the same way we would grieve the loss of a spouse, a loved one, or a friend, we need to grieve the loss of trust from a betrayal. Just as a person can come to love again and remarry, we can recover from betrayal to love and trust again.

To do that, though, we have to admit there has been a loss. We have to admit that we have been hurt and our emotions from that hurt are getting the better of us.

Sometimes people are quick to acknowledge that loss—that they are in pain. More often, however, they fall into denial like I did. That will only work to prolong the healing process.

Denial can take a lot of forms. It can sound like:

"Oh, it wasn't that big of a deal."

"It wasn't really their fault—it was the other person's (or the addiction's, or the circumstances)."

"I can handle it."

"It's just a misunderstanding."

"I don't believe he/she really did that."

"I forgave them, so I can forget about it."

Or any of a myriad of other versions that keep the person from facing reality.

Blaming it on something else doesn't help you process your pain. In fact, it can make it worse. Suddenly, you think that you shouldn't be hurt because it wasn't their fault, so what's wrong with you that you feel hurt?

It's a vicious downward cycle.

Blame is just a deflection. Another form of denial. It's another defense mechanism against the pain. It's a little like saying, "If I can find someone or something to blame, then I know it's not my fault. And if it's not my fault, then my pain isn't real."

It's funny how far our brains will go to try to protect us from shame and humiliation—our conscious minds try to turn them into something else, even if that something else will only delay our healing.

This is why it is common to blame God. Anything but facing the pain and shame for ourselves.

"Why Did God Let This Happen?"

Everybody who experiences deep betrayal more than likely will blame God at some point, particularly if they are Christian. They reason, "Okay, God, You could have had him leave the checkbook in my office one day." Or "You could have let me find the burner phone." Or "Lord, I could have accidentally seen him go into the hotel room."

They are all basically the same question: "Lord, how could You have allowed this to happen to me?"

I think that is the biggest question for people who are betrayed. It is especially true if it is an adult who is just now realizing they were betrayed or abused as a child. It is worse if the abuser was someone in leadership at the church, such as the youth director or Sunday school teacher or a priest. It is easy to blame God because we see them as God's representative and He did not stop them.

"God, I was so innocent. Couldn't You have intervened? Couldn't You have exposed it? Why did You allow this to happen?"

I think, at some level, every single betrayed person asks questions like these. The problem is that they are not very helpful.

It's an odd thing about human nature, but when we are emotionally hurt or have experienced trauma, our subconscious minds often work to protect us in ways that are, in fact, counterproductive.

When we are emotionally hurt or have experienced trauma, our subconscious minds often work to protect us in ways that are counterproductive.

Shame and vulnerability are so toxic to our identities that our subconscious mind does everything it can to avoid them. That is why we often repress the memory of what we experienced in a traumatic childhood event. Short of that, our internal instincts will look for a way to deflect these feelings by blaming someone or something. Or it will try to sweep the incident under the carpet as trivial. These responses happen so naturally that we don't even realize we are doing them.

In the short term, protecting ourselves from the immediate shame can keep us from being completely incapacitated. But in the long run, the quick way to getting our lives back is to face the shame and recognize our vulnerabilities and not let them define us.

One definition of shame is that it is "hate turned inward." But by protecting us from shame, our mind also protects the shame. The longer that happens, the more likely we are to accept it as legitimate. This happens more with children than adults because their rational minds are not as developed, but the process is the same. If we let shame have its way, the natural byproduct is to legitimize it. The end result, though, is to accept that this self-hate is justified because we are really worthless, horrible people.

Hell has no lies more destructive than that one.

The only way to counteract that lie is to confront our pain and our shame and expose them for what they are. We hurt because someone hurt us. We feel shame because we think that betrayal reflects on our value. But it doesn't. At its worst, it may reflect poor judgment about who our associates are. We can learn from the incident and live smarter into the future.

Don't fall into the trap of avoiding the pain and shame

through blame. It doesn't mean we can't express it, but we do need to recognize that it tends to separate us from the very help we need.

God, in His sovereign power, did not set you up to be betrayed. He didn't choose for it to happen. He gave people freedom to choose their actions for themselves, and in that freedom your betrayer chose actions that hurt you.

Honestly, God is just as grieved about it as you are. He wants to help. Don't let the pain you feel cut you off from His help.

And don't let it isolate you from others who want to help either.

That's going to mean using the freedom you have. You're going to have to make some conscious choices to get your life back. The first has to be to confront your pain for what it is and determine to process it rather than obsess over it.

The second is not to let it steal the rest of your loved ones from you.

Processing Your Emotions

As I've already mentioned a couple of times, the pain of betrayal has to be confronted and worked through.

It may not be a perfect illustration, but it's a little like sorting one of those catch-all drawers in your kitchen. You need to dump it out on a table, go through things item by item to identify every piece, sort them into categories, and then find new homes for them. You put them away where they actually belong so you can find them when you need them later.

Ignoring that drawer until it is overflowing doesn't help. Nor does dumping it out and then just stuffing everything back into the drawer.

But that's what a lot of people do with the emotions of betrayal—they let a few emotions out and they get frustrated when they can't quickly figure out what they are. So they just stuff them back in even deeper than before. They instinctively know these things need to be sorted and identified, but they never take the time or find the help to sort them properly.

That's what denial looks like.

Therefore the first real step towards healing is to find a healthy way to dump that drawer of feelings out and start to sort them. That can happen in a number of different ways.

Your Journey to Healing

Some healthy ways of processing your pain are:

Talk with a friend.

If you have a close friend who is willing to sit with you and mostly listen while you process, then see if that person would be open to having coffee together a couple of times a month to let you just vent. (It could be a phone call, as well.) Tell them you are not looking for their approval or sympathy as much as to help you identify what you are feeling and get your life back into a healthy perspective. Let them ask questions, but tell them you're not looking for solutions. You don't need them to counsel as much as just let you get your feelings out so your pain can be processed.

Let me offer a bit of caution here. Choose a friend who is spiritually mature and has their emotions under control. By all means, avoid someone who is working through an emotional issue or their own betrayal. The old expression "misery loves company" is true. Choose someone who loves you and who refuses to unload their problems on top of yours.

Write music, paint, draw, start a story.

Pick up your journal where you recorded some of your feelings. This time, draw a picture or something that helps you express what you are feeling. You might find it helpful to write a song or start writing your own novel where the main character is working through a betrayal.

It is often hard to articulate feelings, which is one of the reasons we have art in the first place. Art expresses emotion and human experiences in ways words often fail. Even just going to a museum to walk through the halls and process what you see can help you start sorting out what's going on in your heart and jumpstart your healing process.

Do some reading about the five stages of grief.

There's a lot of great literature on the five stages of grief: denial and isolation, anger, bargaining, depression, and acceptance. Most people who have lost a loved one go through most, if not all, of these stages, though not necessarily all in the same magnitude or in this specific order.

As we've already discussed, processing betrayal can look at lot like losing a loved one to death, because your trust has been seriously injured, to say the least, and the relationship you had with your betrayer will never be the same again. In a very real sense, it has died, and a new one will need to be developed to replace it.

Talk through these stages with a friend or counselor. What thoughts are you having that might fit into these categories? How are these thoughts helping you heal? How might they be hindering that healing?

Truth to Remember

No good will come from stuffing your anger and pain. Find a way to acknowledge and process it.

Six

ISOLATION

No one ever told me that grief felt so like fear.

—C.S. Lewis

The night Allan found his wife's burner phone is one he will never forget. When he grabbed her purse on their way out for the evening, it just fell out on the floor.

He picked it up and it felt odd not to recognize it. "Honey, whose phone is this?"

"What do you mean?" she asked, walking into the room still fastening an earring. When she saw it, she stopped dead in her tracks.

He looked back at the phone and pressed to open it. It was locked, but the last unread message appeared on the lock screen: "Had the best time yesterday afternoon. Can't get it out of my mind. When can we meet again? Or maybe just go straight to the hotel this time?" The message was punctuated with a wink emoji.

The rest of the evening was a blur. There was a lot of yelling and accusations. The next thing he remembered was sitting on the bed trying to figure out what had happened. He didn't sleep at all that night.

The next time he saw his wife was at the counselor's office. A friend at work had given him the counselor's name. He left a voicemail on his wife's regular phone with the address and time to meet. She, in turn, tried to call him several times, but he hadn't listened to any of the messages she had left.

When she showed up to the meeting late, he could hardly restrain his anger. Somehow, he managed to keep his cool. He let the counselor initiate the conversation, and he set some parameters for their dialogue. But all Allan could think about was "How long has this been going on? Where did you meet him? When? What did you do? How many times did you meet? How long was it before you started sleeping together?" He had questions about every detail, and he felt he deserved to know.

His wife left the office in tears within fifteen minutes.

The counselor was trying to say something to him, but he didn't hear a word of it. He left the office soon after, letting enough time pass to be sure he wouldn't run into his wife in the parking lot.

For the next week he just went between his office and the hotel room where he was staying. The normal things he did every week, usually with his wife, he avoided for fear of running into her. He didn't dare go to any of their usual restaurants. The only call he made was to a private detective who he paid to give him the details of all that his wife and her "friend" had been up to.

While the details he could uncover didn't help, he wanted to learn more. He scoured the internet hoping to maybe find a Facebook photo or something about this guy. When he knew his wife wouldn't be home, he'd sneak in and go through her things. None of that turned up anything. Plus every time he did it, he felt bad about it afterward.

Allan called his brother. But after several minutes of him going through the same few details over and over again, his brother said, "Look, Allan, this is horrible, but I don't know how to help you. I love you, brother, but you need to talk to someone there. I think obsessing over these details is only making it worse. Maybe you should talk with your pastor or something."

Everyone he talked to told him this same thing or found an excuse to get away from him.

It got to the point where if someone said, "It's a beautiful day," he'd respond, "Yeah, like the beautiful day that guy took my wife out for that first boat ride."

Those kinds of comments pretty much ended every conversation anyone started with him.

People were avoiding him in the hallways at work. He'd call people, and they wouldn't pick up or even respond to his voice-mails. After a month or so of this, he finally did reach out and meet with his pastor. He was at the end of his rope.

"Why doesn't anyone care?" he asked his pastor. "Why won't people talk with me anymore?"

Avoiding Isolation

After a betrayal, people often instinctively act in counter-productive ways. The betrayal has revealed that the world they trusted before is not what they thought it was. What else have they missed? Where else might hurt come from?

Who else is deceiving them?

Though we want and need empathy, if we're not careful, these instincts will convince us to act in ways that drive others away—to self-isolate in order to avoid experiencing that pain again.

We can never be hurt again if we are never vulnerable, we reason. So we start building walls that aren't easily torn down. And we don't notice because we are focused on something else.

One of the things I have seen in those I've counseled is that, because the trauma brings the betrayal back to them over and over again, they fall into a paralysis of analysis. They want to know every detail of the betrayal. Knowing the details lets them blame the other person. They want to determine the reason for everything.

And in that process, that's all they talk about. That's exactly what happened to Allan.

His instincts told him that if he could place that blame elsewhere, he could absolve himself of the shame he felt from having been betrayed—a feeling that was misplaced from the start. In the process, he withdrew even further into his obsession and drove people away.

That's a vicious cycle that only prolongs the healing process.

When the Friends You Had Together Are No Longer Your Friends

Dan and Sheryl were both very active socially and they hung out with a handful of couples, including Sheryl's best friend, Sue. Sue's husband, Peter, also happened to be one of Dan's regular golfing buddies, so it was natural for the four of them to get together to barbeque in the summer or when the Steelers were playing, a team both Dan and Peter had rooted for since they were kids. It was a regular thing each fall to flipflop hosting each other for the games.

When Sheryl found out that Dan had been having an affair with a coworker, everything changed. To make matters worse, she found out that Peter and Sue had known about it for months.

To Sheryl, it felt like double betrayal. Not only had her husband been unfaithful, but her best friend had kept the secret from her. Sue tried to defend her silence by saying that Dan promised to tell her. Sue said she thought it would be best coming directly from Dan instead of her telling it. Sue felt like she was between a rock and a hard place having to talk to Sheryl and not tell her while she waited for Dan to confess.

Sheryl didn't buy it.

Dan and Sheryl decided to have a trial separation while Sheryl decided if she wanted to file for divorce or not. Dan had broken off the affair a few months back and had confessed it to her as a mistake and asked for her forgiveness. She didn't know what she was going to do.

What she did know was that Sunday afternoons were a lot lonelier now without the regular festivities for each week's game. Plus she knew Dan was at Peter and Sue's as he had always been. She was alone at home with their kids. They had been open about it, and Sheryl had told them it was fine, but it still stung. She wasn't sure how they could even let Dan into their home after what he had done to her.

She felt like she had lost her husband and her best friend and had no one she could talk to. *Why aren't people mad at him?* she wondered. *Don't people understand what he did?*

Betrayal doesn't happen in a vacuum. The betrayed and the betrayer are not the only ones involved. There are always several

Betrayal can be a lot like a painful injury on your fingertip. It takes only the smallest of brushes with some memory to bring all the pain flooding back.

relationships shared in common, and when we are betrayed, not everyone is going to see things the same way we do.

I had a friend who smashed the tip of his index finger in a door. He reached to shut it and a sudden wind came up and pinched his finger between the door and the door jam. We tend not to think about our fingertips until we smash them. Not only is it painful, but every time it brushes something, we're instantly reminded of the injury. And with the tip of your finger, that's a lot!

I remember him saying to me, "Do you have any idea how many things you touch with the tip of your index finger every day? Smash the end of it and you'll find out. If I sit down, I bump my finger. If I pick something up, I bump my finger. If I take a bite of food, I bump my finger against the plate. It was so painful at first, but as the weeks went by, I could bump more things and it hurt less and less."

Betrayal can be a lot like a painful injury on your fingertip. It takes only the smallest of brushes with some memory to bring all the pain flooding back. We relive the shock of first learning about the betrayal over and over again.

When we experience the trauma of a betrayal, our minds go into protection mode, just as they would if we were assaulted by someone. If you've ever been robbed or had your house broken into when you weren't home, you know the feeling of violation that comes with it. You don't want to ever feel that exposed and vulnerable again.

You become hypervigilant. You buy an early warning security system for your home and car. You are on the alert for suspicious characters or behavior. You're going to protect yourself so you never have to feel like that again.

In the same way, when you get betrayed your subconscious mind starts to look for threats of betrayal everywhere. You suspect everyone. You start to examine every close relationship you have for signs of deceit. You withdraw from contact with others. You become more guarded in what you say and how close others can get to you.

This isn't a conscious decision. It's just something we do instinctually. And if we're not careful, it can leave us completely on our own—or worse.

Keeping the Right People Out and Letting the Wrong People In

Another thing I have witnessed is even more alarming, and it stems from our need to put our identities back together after a betrayal. There is a stigma to being betrayed, even if it is mostly self-imposed. It's easy to want to avoid that feeling by replacing too quickly the person who has left—especially if the new person affirms our feelings and tells us what we want to hear.

There has also been a sudden loss of intimacy. I don't mean sexually, though that is often true as well, but emotionally. Someone we deeply trusted and relied upon is no longer in our lives. We often want to fill that void as quickly as possible.

In such cases, it's not only our trust that is a casualty, but also our rationality. As we become hesitant to trust others, sometimes we trust ourselves too much.

If we don't balance that with people who we know will tell us the truth, like a longtime friend or trusted counselor, we can fall prey to people who want to take advantage of our pain.

You don't have to watch *Dr. Phil* for long to see an episode about a widow or widower being conned out of thousands of dollars by someone on the internet. The person meets them on social media. They start chatting together. The other person says all the right things, building intimacy and trust with a veneer of lies. Then they tell them they need money for a surgery they can't afford. Or they tell them about a "sure thing" business they can invest in. Or they need money to take care of a loved one.

The person supposedly lives thousands of miles away (I say "supposedly" because a lot of times the online personality is completely fictional), which provides a safety of sorts. The person can be open with them without risking them actually knowing them.

Over time they build a relationship that is based on repairing the betrayed person's identity and sense of intimacy by constantly telling them how wonderful they are and things that make them feel good about themselves.

Or maybe there was a person in business whose partner turned on them and left their company bankrupt. An "investor" comes along with an opportunity to triple their money in ninety days. The guy is driving a Jaguar and seems to know what he's doing. He'd put up all of the money himself, but he just doesn't have the cash at the moment.

You see, he went through the same thing. His partner took everything, and he went bankrupt, just like the businessperson. But now he has found this better mousetrap and it's a "sure thing." All he needs is to find someone who can get his hands on the cash.

Isolated from the business community this businessperson had come to know over the years and hungry to make lost money back, this businessperson invests the rest of their family's retirement nest egg only to eventually learn the guy was a con artist and a thief. Wanting to get back their cash and reputation in one fell swoop, they open themselves up to even further betrayal and pain.

Betrayal makes us susceptible to people who agree with our pain and side with us, even if they are only saying those things to betray us themselves.

Normally, without the pain from the betrayal we just went through, we would know to be more suspicious when we hear things that sound too good to be true. But in our pain, in our desire to repair our egos and reputation, we lose part of our ability to filter input. We turn down our truth detectors in favor of accepting whatever we hear that is affirming.

"I can't believe anyone would risk losing someone as beautiful as you."

"You know, after my boyfriend left me, I never thought I'd find someone I could trust again—until I met you."

"That's a horrible break. What a crook!"

They're telling us how wonderful we are, that they see things others have never seen in us. And for the first time somebody agrees with everything we say. Why? Because they're lying. They just want us to trust them so that they can manipulate us. But we are looking so hard for approval or something to fill the empty place in us by the betrayal that we fall for it hook, line, and sinker.

This is another reason why, in the midst of betrayal, we need to cling to the relationships that have been with us for a long time—family, friends, leaders in our faith communities. We need to find the relationships that helped define us before we met the betrayer.

Those are often the best people to help us deal with our new reality. People who will be honest with us even if it hurts. But who, at the same time, care enough to always speak truth in love to us. People who will help us put our egos and lives back together at a more natural and lasting pace.

"I'm Never Going to Trust Again"

The emotions we feel when we are betrayed have a tendency to color everything around us. Where we before saw safety and reliability, we now question. "If I was blind to the lies and deceit of my betrayer, who else is fooling me?"

We feel like the easiest way to protect ourselves from the pain is to withdraw into ourselves and never extend trust again.

But that is no way to live.

The greatest joys in life come from relationships—things like the birth of a child, winning a game with a team, family gatherings and holidays, our colleagues who work with us trying to change the world. Good things can happen from private alone time, but even they will mean little if they can never be shared.

As any marriage counselor or therapist will tell you, *always* and *never* are dangerous words. "Never trusting again" is only going to seal you into the misery you are experiencing in the wake of your betrayal. The only way out is to either rebuild your relationship—if the betrayer is truly repentant and willing to go through the work of proving it—or build better relationships somewhere else.

Alone is not only no way to live, but it also keeps you from healing.

To step out of denial and isolation is to step out of the initial shock of your betrayal and into the emotional aftermath of it. It's to acknowledge the pain and release the anger of the unfairness of what has just happened to you—the wrath you have for the partner or friend who broke the contract of your relationship and violated your trust in them. It's to let loose all the emotions caused by what happened and let the bomb of your broken heart explode.

Alone is not only no way to live, but it also keeps you from healing.

Only after that can you start picking up and putting back together all the pieces. This is the next stage you will experience in processing the grief caused by your betrayal.

Once you have overcome your denial and emerged from your isolation, it's time to manage your anger and other emotions that come with it.

It's time to "let it all out." Processing your feelings is the next part of your journey to healing.

Your Journey to Healing

Isolation can make you feel like the world revolves around what happened to you. Here are some things you can try to help keep you from being isolated and having everything distorted and out of proportion.

Choose a specific time you will talk about your feelings and what happened to you, and then turn it off the rest of the day.

You'll likely still think about it, but recognize the rest of the world isn't thinking about it the same way you are. Talking about it in passing with a colleague at work is not the same as writing about it in your journal or talking with your pastor.

You will have your time to talk about it in detail in a helpful way. Recognize that talking about it outside of that setting is unlikely to do anyone any good.

It may sound odd, but one of the reasons counseling is effective is that there is a set time to begin and a set time to end. And you and your counselor both focus on the issue when you are together. When you leave the office, you can leave what was discussed there behind.

Socialize face-to-face with other people.

Even if you just need someone to sit or walk with you, find ways to get out and be with other people. Go to church, be a part of a Bible study group, join a club or exercise group. While sitting alone with your thoughts is probably needed at times, don't fall into the trap of isolating yourself and alienating those who care about you.

We're not designed to go through life alone, and we certainly aren't meant to deal with our trauma and stresses alone. If nothing else, get out of your house and go for a walk in the middle of the day. Go watch kids play at the park. Eat lunch with other people at work. Make sure you don't separate yourself from the more normal world where life goes on and people trust one another in relative safety.

If you are feeling overwhelmed by emotion, ask before you start unloading your feelings on another person.

Again, this is better done with a close friend rather than a stranger or acquaintance, but before you verbally vomit your feelings all over another person, ask if they would mind listening to something very personal for a few minutes without needing to give feedback.

Friends will often give us that space. If they don't, it is all right. It doesn't mean they don't care about you. Some people who love you aren't comfortable listening to your struggles. Plus you don't know what they are going through themselves. Your extra sharing might not be good for them at the time.

When friends ask you to do things, go!

It's often not easy to create ways to be with friends when you are hurting, and the last thing you feel like doing is asking them to go out, so make it easy on yourself—don't turn them down when they reach out to do something with you. Not everything has to be about processing your pain.

A great deal of good is done by just getting out of your own space and seeing a world where not everything has been tainted by betrayal. Get out and live!

Truth to Remember

Healthy relationships are essential to your future. Don't let a betrayal keep you from people. Socialize!

Seven

ANGER

*Anger is an acid that can do more harm to the vessel in which it is
stored than to anything on which it is poured.*

—MARK TWAIN

Emily was a beautiful young woman who came for prayer at one of our events. She was engaged to a young man she dearly loved. They were planning to marry the next month. All of this seemed so wonderful.

Why was she coming for prayer?

"I think there's something wrong with me," she said. "We kiss and we hold hands, but I can't get comfortable with him hugging me or touching me any more than that. I don't know what to do. The thought of our wedding night together brings up so much anxiety, I want to call off the wedding."

To make a long story shorter, our staff suggested Emily see a counselor. She did. In talking with her, memories from her childhood resurfaced that threw her into a panic. When she was very young, she had been sexually molested by her grandfather who had recently passed away.

Now she also understood why she couldn't bring herself to go to his funeral. The realization turned her world upside down. Everything about her childhood now seemed tainted. She suddenly looked on everyone with suspicion.

Had anyone known? Her grandmother? Her cousins? Her parents?

No one suspected anything?

Why had he been allowed to babysit her? Why was she left alone with him? Was she the only victim? How had all of this been repressed for all of these years?

She spoke with her fiancé about it. They decided to postpone the wedding and go to counseling together. He was very supportive. She was so grateful.

If only it had been the same with her family.

Her father was in denial. "My father would never have done anything like that."

Her mother was aghast. It drove a spike between her and her husband. And she was angry with herself. She couldn't believe she hadn't seen the signs.

Her uncle, her father's brother, was outraged at the accusation. "He's not here to defend himself. How can we take your word for this? I don't think you're remembering things right. It must've been someone else. Or maybe you're just making the whole thing up."

Her grandmother told yet another story. "I know he had some

indiscretions when he was younger, but I thought he'd grown past all of that. I'm so sorry dear. I never thought…he was a different man when he passed away."

Every time she walked into church now, where her grandfather had also attended, people looked at her differently. Some would see her and head the other direction. Others didn't seem to know how to talk with her. A smaller group of people looked down their noses at her like she was damaged goods.

Emily was so angry she could hardly see straight—and she was angry with good reason. But it didn't seem to be helping anything. She felt like she was falling down a rabbit hole wanting a revenge she knew she would never get.

She had a lot of emotions to work through.

The Reason for Anger

Anger is a natural reaction to things that could harm us or that violate our sense of justice—what is right and fair—in our world.

Anger—and other core emotions like fear, disgust, and surprise—are hardwired into us. We don't have to consciously decide to be angry. It just happens.

This is good when our lives are at stake or something happens that might harm us. When we get angry, adrenaline is pumped into our systems. We instantly are more alert, ready for action, and motivated to take on whatever challenge is in front of us.

If we are in immediate physical danger, getting angry can mean the difference between life and death. It can give us a quicker reaction to swerve out of danger when someone cuts us off in traffic or give us the extra jolt of speed and aggression we need to succeed in a sport.

Believe it or not, psychologists tell us that anger can actually increase our optimism, creativity, and make us more effective and motivated in what we are trying to accomplish.[5] It can encourage us to support a cause and inspire us to change the world.

Of course, anger also has a downside. The same instinctive reaction that could save our lives in one situation could seriously injure an innocent bystander or someone we love in another. This is especially true with emotions. A continually angry boss in a workplace can wreak havoc on employees. A spouse with a short fuse can destroy the sanctity of a home, especially if anger leads to abuse.

As the old saying goes, "Anger is only one letter away from danger." We need to realize that anger is a God-given emotion for our protection, but it can also be acted upon to great harm.

Everything God designed for our good, the devil tries to get us to abuse and distort. When we do, what was meant for good harms us. Anger is no exception.

As Benjamin Franklin said, "Whatever's begun in anger ends in shame," and "Anger is never without a reason, but it seldom has a good one."

Because of its dangers, some people try to avoid anger altogether. They repress their anger instead of expressing it. That isn't a healthy option either.

There are long-term dangers when we stuff our anger. Repressed anger shows up as stress in our bodies. It can lead to anything between a sleepless night and a fatal heart attack, depending on how long and how deeply we repress it.

Long-term repressed anger will turn to bitterness that will discolor the way we see the world. It will affect how we relate to people. It will corrode our well-being. It can literally poison and shorten our lives.

Long-term repressed
anger will turn to
bitterness that will discolor
the way we see the world.
It will affect how we relate
to people. It will corrode
our well-being.

Bitterness is exactly what I experienced when I repressed my anger over my friend's betrayal. I lost my passion for the ministry. It stole the joy of living from me, even though I have a good number of reasons to be pleased with my life.

Dealing with My Anger

One of the first things my counseling friend asked me when we met was how the betrayal had made me feel.

"Well, as you know, it's been a couple of years now," I said.

"Yes," he said, "but when it first happened, how did you react?"

It took us a while to see that after the surprise and shock, it made me really angry. Honestly, I had a hard time admitting it. For one thing, I felt like getting angry wasn't the response a Christian should have. I didn't think it was spiritual.

Closely related was my unwillingness to admit that he had gotten to me. I wanted to shrug it off as if it wasn't a big deal.

"I want you to know you need to give yourself permission to be angry about what happened," he told me. "Anger is a natural reaction to injustice or evil. God gets angry. In fact, Jesus got angry when He went to the temple and saw what was supposed to be a place of prayer turned into a noisy marketplace. And He even acted on His anger to clear the place and chastise the merchants who were corrupting the space.

"Now, I don't think you should be chasing anyone around with a whip, but you need to give yourself permission to be angry so that you can process it. You remember that Paul wrote that we should be angry and sin not? Well, in the same verse he said that we shouldn't let the sun go down on our anger. [See Ephesians 4:26.] That means you should start dealing with it the moment you sense the anger inside of you. Occasionally you will find the anger may return the next day, but you just have to keep confronting it and dealing with it.

"You need to feel it and let it wash over you. You need to think about what caused it. You need to express it in a healthy way. Only then will you be able to release it."

We had to meet a couple of times before I was really able to do that. He taught me that I could be upset in a healthy way—that my anger was an indicator of something I needed to speak out or do something about. If I was angry, it was better if I expressed it in an honest way that didn't attack the character of the other person—in a way that wasn't lashing out. I could state it this way, "When you did such and such, it really made me mad." That way I'm not attacking the person but the issue.

Sometimes when we do that, we find out we totally misinterpreted the situation and shouldn't have reacted as we did. Sometimes we realize the other person had no idea that what they did was upsetting to us. And almost every time, we learn something about ourselves.

Why did I get angry about that when it didn't bother anyone else? Why was it an affront to me? What is it about how I see myself that that so challenged?

Or is there something in this situation that is inherently wrong that shouldn't be allowed to continue? Is there a more righteous, just way to do things, one that better respects the personal integrity and dignity of all involved?

Or is there something I should change about my character? About the way I behave? Emotions aren't evil. We are made in the image of God, and we have emotions because God has emotions. We love, we feel joy, we get angry because something happens that touches part of our soul and we react.

How we react, however, is important. When we react without leaving a space to consider what's going on between the emotion we feel and the reaction it inspires, that is when we get into trouble. That's when anger jumps to danger.

Simply noticing what we are feeling and asking ourselves why before we react can make all the difference in the world.

Though I can't prove it from Scripture, I think Jesus did exactly that before He cleared the temple of moneychangers and peddlers. He knew asking nicely wouldn't change the hearts of people who were making money where the only commerce should be with God. Thus He made a ruckus that would get the attention of the elders and force the people to think twice before setting up their stalls again.

He was driving them from their own unrighteousness. He was holding them accountable for their actions and asking them to do things a different, holier way.

There are things happening today that should make us very, very angry. When I hear about human trafficking, it infuriates me. When I see pornography destroy a marriage, I get livid. When I see addiction of one sort or another threaten to destroy a life, it enrages me.

Those are God-inspired emotions that are there to motivate me to do something. I then have a choice of reacting to that in a healthy or unhealthy way.

I could physically attack the people that I think represent this unrighteousness, but that would more likely result in getting me arrested than stopping evil.

Or I could find a more positive way to address the issue that is angering me. I could give money to an organization working to bring human traffickers to justice and rescue the people caught in its grips. I could speak out to raise social awareness. I could volunteer to help at a halfway house where people can get help.

There are a lot of positive things I could do and should do as soon as possible. I shouldn't let them just pass by me and harden my heart before the sun goes down. God wants us to get mad at injustice and do something about it—something that He would condone and is in accordance with how He loves the world. He wants us to channel our anger into positive action. To do as Paul said: to "overcome evil with good" (Romans 12:21).

Be Angry and Do Not Sin

Giving myself permission to be angry gave me an opportunity to deal with other emotions I experienced because of the betrayal. When we stuff the most powerful emotion we feel, we also stuff the emotions beneath it.

When I was able to acknowledge my anger, I was also able to deal with the shame I felt at being deceived and gullibly accepting his first repentance as genuine. I could deal with the guilt that I felt for failing to see his insincerity. As the old saying goes, "Fool me once: shame on you. Fool me twice; shame on me."

I also was able to recognize how my stuffed anger came out in other ways—the broiling dissatisfaction I felt in general.

How I refused to get close to people I worked with for fear they might one day betray me as well.

I projected the betrayal of one person onto dozens if not hundreds of others. Not only was that unfair to them, it was eating away at my soul. It was also hurting the effectiveness of my work and affecting the relationships in my family.

Unexpressed and unprocessed anger and emotions have a way of coming out in all the wrong ways and masking what we should

Unexpressed and unprocessed anger and emotions have a way of coming out in all the wrong ways and masking what we should really be addressing.

really be addressing. It has a way of compounding our hurt into a number of other arenas. For me, the effects were fairly mild, but for others they can be severe.

Unprocessed emotions can lead to a world of harm. It's often said that "Hurt people hurt people." That only happens when people don't process their hurts and work toward forgiveness.

Once I gave myself permission to express and release my anger, I realized there were other benefits. I found I wasn't so argumentative any more, having to always prove to everyone I was right. That applied to the betrayal and asking for the resignation of my friend, of course—though I never went into great details when explaining to others what had happened—but also about unrelated things. Having been wronged made me constantly need to justify that I was in the right. It was a strange obsession.

Letting go of that was a real healing point for me. Not always having to get everyone to agree with me changed the nature of a lot of my relationships.

I didn't need to control everything and everyone around me to prevent being hurt again.

Another release was I was able to stop denying how the betrayal had affected me. I never denied that it happened, but I did deny that it bothered me. I was pretending that it rolled off me like water off a duck's back, but inside I had been hurt. Denying that hurt was just stuffing more emotions and continuing the bad cycle that was sucking the joy out of my life.

As I began processing all of these things one by one, I was able to see that the responsibility for the betrayal was not mine to own. I subconsciously had been believing that the betrayal was my fault. My friend's bad actions did not reflect my value as a person or my competence as a minister.

Yes, the action was towards me, but it didn't make me a lesser person.

It didn't mean God loved me any less. It didn't mean my ministry was going to go down the tubes if anyone found out what had happened—that his actions didn't reflect who we were as an organization.

His failure did not mean I was a failure. But that's not how I felt.

As I dug deeper, I realized that my anger wasn't all focused on my friend's actions or betrayal. I was also angry at myself. I was upset that I had let myself be duped. I felt like someone had tattooed "stupid" on my forehead for all to see.

That was a feeling I didn't want to confront.

It wasn't until I did, though, that I started to get freedom. I didn't actually forgive myself for it, but I did have to acknowledge I was fallible, and that I needed to add checks and balances in our organization to prevent something like that from ever happening again.

I had to come to peace with the idea that I was only human.

I know that might seem obvious or sound a little simple to you as you read it. But all of this kind of stuff really did go through my mind—that somehow one bad actor was going to taint all the good we were doing and wanted to do. It didn't mean others would not betray me later. Or that people with hidden motives wouldn't be able to sneak in and do harm the same way he had. But now we could watch out for it and have a plan for how to deal with it.

To walk biblically and spiritually through all of my emotions helped me to understand the most important relationship I have is the one with my Lord and Savior, Jesus Christ. Having been betrayed revealed the chinks in the armor of that relationship. That betrayal had made me doubt how much He loved me and question His goodness.

I came to understand that as long as that relationship was healthy and growing, then I could have other healthy relationships, no matter what other people did to me.

In fact, I came to realize if my relationship with my heavenly Father was healthy and maturing, then I could handle all the unhealthy relationships that came my way. When we accept that He loves us and we are "accepted in the Beloved" (Ephesians 1:6 NKJV), then we can be spiritually, emotionally, and physically able to make it through any human betrayal.

You Don't Owe Anyone an Explanation

As you begin to process your anger and other emotions, remember that you're not obligated to discuss with anyone the details of your betrayal. I know sometimes it is a temptation. Coworkers, family, and friends want to know particulars because of curiosity and especially because they love gossip! The attention you receive can feel good for a while. But you must remind yourself often that not everyone asking about what happened has your best interests in mind. Most of the time they are just after a juicy story.

I know from experience that people who are too free with this information usually regret letting too many people in on the details. It is better to disclose such information in the office of a counselor who is sworn to confidentiality or to a close friend who you know isn't the town gossip.

After you've had some time to go over the details with someone you trust, you'll want to determine how much you can share and who should hear it. You might have a short version you can develop with your confidant. But you don't owe anyone, especially just a curious acquaintance, the whole story.

I say this because I know people will ask. People still ask today, over twenty years later, about what happened to me. When someone asks my staff, they are unsure how to respond. Most of them know few, if any, details about it.

When asked, out of respect for the man's family, I share only the few details most people already know. Beyond that, I use a line I learned from my federal agent friends: "I'm not at liberty to say."

When We Don't Process Our Emotions

When we fail to address our emotions in a healthy way, they are going to find a way to come out anyway—often in ways we don't realize until it's too late, in ways that are harmful to us and those around us. Here are a few of the things I've noticed that happen when emotions aren't dealt with openly and directly.

We become argumentative.

Stuffed emotions eat away at the foundations of our self-identity. We end up constantly having to prove ourselves. We can become opinionated monsters no one wants around, driving us further into isolation and making us even more disagreeable.

We can become shallow.

Rather than grounding our self-worth on solid truth—such as what God thinks of us and how much He loves us—we cling to shallower "wins." We try to get everyone to agree on an issue we believe in or to seek accolades by preaching to the choir, condemning people or groups who aren't there to defend their positions.

One way this shallowness comes out is when we start drawing a question mark over the character of everyone we encounter, not only in our minds but in the minds of others. If a friend speaks favorably about someone, we feel the need to respond by saying things like, "I've got a feeling she is not the person you think she is," or "That is not what I heard." And we say these things even when we have no basis for our opinion.

We displace or transfer our emotions.

When we don't process our anger toward a betrayer, we can project it elsewhere, as I did with church leadership or those who disagreed with me. It was easier to be angry at a nebulous group than deal with my specific issues.

We become bitter and stress destroys our happiness.

Hebrews 12:15 states that if we let bitterness take root in our hearts it will "cause trouble" and defile many. Bitter roots spring into bitter fruit. And if we don't uproot it, it will spread.

Emotional hurt is real. It doesn't go away on its own or without a healing process.

When we feel physical pain, one of the first steps is to go to urgent care or the emergency room, depending on the severity. Often a specific incident or accident caused the pain, such as a fall or a collision. Once the doctor has seen us, they will prescribe a drug or some kind of therapy. They may refer us to a specialist for further investigation. In most cases, they can offer a remedy and a path to wholeness, which usually involves steps we need to take.

"Leave this cast on for six weeks."

"Alternate icing it and putting on a hot pad for the next eight hours."

"Take two aspirin and call me in the morning."

If it's anything significant, it's going to take some time to heal.

Emotional healing is similar. But emotional healing is not as outwardly evident as walking around with crutches and a cast on our leg. It is still going to take some time, though. There is likely some kind of therapy or counseling we should plug in to so that the healing comes quicker and will keep us from getting reinjured anytime soon.

As I tell many people who come to me with emotional hurt, "Your first goal is to get through today. Take it one day at a time."

Your Journey to Healing

There are many healthy ways to process the emotions you are feeling and channel your rage in a constructive direction. In the next few days, try these:

Express your feelings in prayer.

I often tell people the best place to vent your anger is to the Lord. He already knows it anyway. Don't obsess about it, but do tell God how you feel. The Book of Psalms is filled with people pouring their heart and frustrations out to God in prayer. When we have pain in our lives, it can be incredibly helpful to pray over the Psalms and realize we are not alone.

It also is helpful to read stories from the Bible of people who cried out to God and expressed their thoughts and feelings. The Israelites, for example, cried out to God for deliverance. Job did as well and, despite his bluntness, God vindicated him in front of his friends.

Insert a pause between your emotion and your response to others because if it.

The old advice about counting to ten before responding when you are angry is good advice. That remedy is not about the counting but about giving yourself time to choose a more rational response.

Abraham Lincoln is one of my favorite leaders in American history. The way he interacted with people—his critics, his family, and other leaders—is an example for all of us to follow. One thing in particular that impresses me about Lincoln is the way he handled anger. If Abraham Lincoln had to write to someone when he was angry with them, he would write two letters. In the first, he let out all his frustrations and insults. He would hold nothing back. Once he got it all out, he'd tear that up and write a second one that was more diplomatic and godlier.

Continue writing in your journal or writing poetry or song lyrics.

If you started doing any of these things I suggested in earlier chapters, keep going! Apply what you have read. And be creative. If you find another way to explore and express your feelings in a healthy way, do it. The more you write, draw, or sing, the more your emotions will come in line with reality.

Avoid other people who are angry.

Sometimes, especially if you are part of a group that's been betrayed by a leader or someone in the group, all people want to talk about when they are together are the details of what happened. This is one of the reasons the Bible is so hard on gossip. It's like pouring gasoline on a fire. Being part of such conversations is not a healthy way to process anger or disappointment.

Truth to Remember

Anger isn't wrong, but it is a warning sign that something isn't right in your world. It's there to alert you for your protection. Staying on alert for too long and acting under that pressure is where problems often occur. Assess your situation, control your responses, and act constructively.

Eight

....

FORGIVENESS

*As I walked out the door toward the gate that would
lead to my freedom, I knew if I didn't leave my bitterness
and hatred behind, I'd still be in prison.*

—NELSON MANDELA

Joyce was a longtime friend of the family. We were excited
when she married Ben. They appeared to be the perfect couple. However, some six years and two children into their marriage, we learned that Joyce had left her husband and was filing
for divorce.

Once the divorce was finalized, she came to me for advice.

"About three years into our marriage," she told me, "Ben had
a rough patch at work and started drinking. He didn't seem to
be any kind of drinker when we dated, but he may have been, I
don't know. He'd never talk about it.

"When he drank, he'd get angry. At first, he smashed some things in the house. It was upsetting, but it was just stuff. We talked about it, and he agreed not to drink anymore. But that lasted only a few weeks.

"The next time he drank, I confronted him about it, and that was the first time he hit me. I was shocked, grabbed the kids and left the house. He was just a different person—it was like some kind of beast came out when he drank.

"I came back the next day and he apologized. He promised he wouldn't drink anymore, and we got rid of all the alcohol in the house. I thought it was something we could fix.

"I urged him to get counseling, but he said he'd be all right. Things were better at work now and he didn't need to drink anymore. We'd get through it.

"Despite his promise, I was continually on edge when he was home. I tried to casually smell his breath whenever he'd come home late in case he'd been to a bar or bought something and drank it on the way home. It was hard to tell. A couple of times I was sure he'd had a couple of drinks, but he denied it.

"I wasn't sure what to do."

She paused, studying her fingertips.

"Then one night he came home late and I was in the kitchen still making dinner. He flew into a rage that dinner wasn't already on the table. I told him I'd fed the kids and was just waiting for him to come home. This just made things worse.

"He raced at me and threw the boiling pan of spaghetti sauce across the room just as our son, Jeremy, was coming in. Some of it splashed onto his arm and he screamed. Ben screamed at me again and tried to slap me.

"I grabbed both kids and rushed Jeremy to the hospital to have them look at the burn. When I told them what had happened, I was sent to a counselor and the police were sent to our house. That's when I realized things had gone too far.

"Ben and I separated, we went to counseling, but in the end, he couldn't convince me he wouldn't drink again. He couldn't convince our counselor either. That's when I asked for the divorce. I was heartbroken, but it was the only way I knew I could keep the kids safe.

"Ben got visitation rights, all contingent on him getting counseling and attending AA meetings. He came to me and was so apologetic. Every time he picks up the kids, I'm scared though. He seems all right and to be doing better, but I know it only takes one night to have everything blow up again.

"I'm trying to forgive him for what's happened, and I feel like I have. I want him to get better, but I still don't trust him with the kids. Now he's asking if the kids can come over and stay with him on the weekends. He's made rooms for them in his new place. But I don't know.

"I talked with a friend of mine, and she said if I'd really forgiven him then I would forget what he'd done before and give him a chance. That's what God does, after all. He forgives and casts our sin into the sea of forgetfulness. But I'm scared for the kids. Jeremy still has a mark on his arm from the burns. I don't know what to do.

"I really want to forgive him for what he has done. I've moved on with my life, but I just can't forget what he did when he drank."

She looked up at me for the first time since she started talking. Her eyes were glistening. "Am I a bad person that I can't forget what he did to Jeremy? If I really forgive Ben for what he did, does that mean I have to risk him hurting the kids again?"

The Real Meaning of Forgiveness

Joyce wasn't the first person to ask me questions like those.

I've had businessmen ask me if forgiving an employee or a vendor for doing something illegal or unethical meant they had to restore the relationship and give them their job back.

I've had people ask me if forgiving someone who gossiped about them meant they had to trust that person with personal information about themselves again.

I've had women ask me if forgiveness meant they had to reconcile with their spouse even though they experienced verbal and physical abuse.

I think all of these come from a fundamental misunderstanding of what forgiveness really means.

"Do I have to interact with that person again?"

"How do I deal with them if I can't avoid being around them?"

"Does it mean I shouldn't be checking up on what they promised to change? Should I make sure they are seeing their counselor? To make sure they're dealing with their addiction?"

"Do I have to act like nothing ever happened?"

Apparently we get the idea that forgiving means you totally forget about what happened. If what happened ever comes to your mind, you haven't forgiven the offender. If you think about it, you haven't forgiven. These ideas may be idealistic but they aren't realistic. And that leads us to believe that forgiving someone means believing the violation never happened in the first place. It means you have to reconcile, restore trust, and rebuild your relationship with that person.

The most common word for forgiveness used in the New Testament also translates as "leave" or "suffer." The second most common word translates "pardon." These mean to relinquish what is owed, as in forgiving a debt or pardoning a criminal. It means that you will not "prosecute" them for what they did. You are giving up the right to "press charges." You're giving up the right to seek vengeance against that person.

What it doesn't mean is, "You broke into my house and stole my things. I forgive you. Here are my keys. Go in and take whatever you want."

God forgives and forgets because what He forgives will never be counted against that person again. It is not, however, a license to go out and sin again.

Do you remember the woman caught in adultery that the Pharisees brought to Jesus? Do you remember how Jesus responded? You see, when Jesus forgave a person, it always addressed something in the past. As He told the woman caught in adultery: "Neither do I condemn you; go, and from now on sin no more" (John 8:11). He forgave her sin but instructed her to never fall for that temptation again.

But wait! Didn't Jesus say, "Do not resist the one who is evil. But if anyone slaps you on the right cheek, turn to him the other also" (Matthew 5:39)? Doesn't that mean we have to make ourselves vulnerable again?

Yes, it does. But Jesus isn't talking about forgiveness here, but love. In the context of this verse, He is talking about nonviolent resistance against the occupying Roman army. He is saying that forgiving gives up the right to "an eye for an eye and a tooth for a tooth" (Matthew 5:38). Jesus was teaching us to overcome another's evil actions with good by refusing to strike back and showing we're willing to suffer for what is right.

He's talking about the kind of aggressive love that He demonstrated by being willing to go to the cross to save humanity.

Forgiveness means I am going to give up my right to punish you for what you did to me in the past.

He wasn't talking about the love within a marriage, a friendship, or a partnership. And He certainly wasn't talking about making ourselves a doormat for others to wipe their feet on. Those contexts are different.

Accountability is not unforgiveness. It is a way for us to hold others—and ourselves—to an agreed upon standard of behavior. Strict accountability is crucial to restoring trust. Without it, the relationship cannot be reconciled.

Forgiveness certainly does not mean I have to open myself up to be hurt by the betrayer again. And it certainly doesn't mean Joyce should knowingly put her children in harm's way. It doesn't mean I welcome you back into my trust so that you can hurt me again. That, you will have to earn.

Forgiveness means I am going to give up my right to punish you for what you did to me in the past. I'm not going to look for opportunities to hurt you. I'm giving up my right to retaliate or seek further vengeance.

But I'm not going to let you treat me badly again, either. I respect myself too much for that.

You Can't Love Others If You Don't Love Yourself

What is the second great commandment? "You shall love your neighbor as yourself" (Matthew 22:39).

What is the Golden Rule? "Whatever you wish that others would do to you, do also to them" (Matthew 7:12).

There is a part of these verses that people miss. I cannot love my neighbor in a healthy way until I have a proper self-love. In both places, the basis for loving others is knowing how to love yourself. If you don't care how people treat you, then your standards will be low for how you treat others. How you love yourself sets that standard.

It's very hard to love well if you don't believe that your love means anything. It has to come from a place of self-respect—a place of awareness that you are a creation of God with a unique, God-given purpose. It has to have its roots in knowing your life matters. It is realizing that you are someone special and important to God.

Don't misunderstand what I am saying. A healthy self-love isn't egotistical. Egotistical people are insecure people who can't accept true love. But a healthy self-love means knowing that you are worth something and you deserve the same respect as anyone else.

No one has the right to harm you without you defending yourself. No one has the right to belittle you.

A good rule of thumb to follow is this: if you wouldn't allow someone else to be treated a certain way, you shouldn't let others treat you that way either.

Joyce knew it was wrong to risk letting her husband throw a fit and harm her children. She also knew she didn't deserve to be beaten because her husband couldn't control his temper when he was drinking. If he refused to stop drinking, the best thing was to remove them from the situation.

The problem is a lot of people don't love themselves enough to stand up for themselves like Joyce did.

Perhaps a better way to think of it might be to consider what you would let someone do to your ninety-five-year-old neighbor. If you heard a commotion in their yard and come out to find someone trying to force their way into your neighbor's home, what would you do?

Or if you saw someone trying to get your neighbor's six-year-old into a car against their will, what would you do?

Well, anything you would potentially prevent from happening to them, you should also keep from happening to you. You wouldn't let them be robbed. You wouldn't let them be abused. You wouldn't let them be molested. Nor would you let anyone speak to them harshly or threaten them. If that's the case, why would you let someone do that to you?

I know people struggle with this because they don't value themselves enough. They think they have to "forgive" and put up with their mate's abuse or infidelity or someone's betrayal of them. They often quote the words of Jesus when He was on the cross, "Father, forgive them, for they know not what they do" (Luke 23:34).

Others point to Stephen, the early church leader that was stoned to death (see Acts 7).

These situations, however, are different. The death of Jesus was part of God's plan of redemption. Stephen was a martyr for his faith. Like many Christians who die for their faith today, he was being persecuted by those in authority. Fighting against them was useless. His greatest testimony was to show them he didn't fear death through his nonviolent resistance. As we know from history, such love can overcome armies.

Within our households, though, God expects us to protect ourselves and our loved ones. He expects us to stand up for ourselves and stand against wrongdoing and harming the innocent.

Forgiveness does not mean open the gate for people to hurt or betray us again.

And it doesn't mean we let people get away with murder, either. In some cases, it just means we release the other party to the hands of God.

Revenge Isn't as Sweet as It Appears

The most incredible story of forgiveness I have ever heard was shared by one of our good friends, Debbie Morris, in her book *Forgiving the Dead Man Walking*. Debbie has spoken at several of our conferences and always makes an impact. Her story is nothing short of miraculous.

When Debbie was sixteen, she was kidnapped and brutally raped by serial killer Robert Lee Willie, subject of the movie *Dead Man Walking*. The night she was taken, she was on a date, and her kidnappers left her date for dead. The kidnappers shot him, cut his throat, and tried to hang him before leaving him. Somehow, he lived.

Willie wasn't alone, so after that he let his partner rape her. Then he took her to some of his friends, who also had their way with her. He told her repeatedly that he was going to kill her. He actually said that killing her would be better. That way, she wouldn't have to live with the memories of that night.

Then, for some unexplained reason, at about 4:30 or 5:00 the next morning, Willie pulled over to the side of the road and told Debbie to get out. She was sure it was her end.

Instead of shooting her, however, he just drove away. She was the only victim he allowed to live.

You can understand why it might have been hard for Debbie to forgive Willie for what he did to her. It was horrific.

Not only that, but everyone knew what had happened to her. No boy would date her after that. More than once she wondered if she would have been better off if he had killed her, but she persevered, living for the day she could see her attacker pay for what he had done to her.

She hated him and longed to see him executed.

Thanks to her testimony and other evidence, Willie and his accomplice were eventually captured and put on trial. They discovered several other crimes Willie committed. The trial was arduous and long. Eventually, he was found guilty and sentenced to die in the electric chair.

Then came all the appeals and pleas for stays of execution. Though all were denied, it would be ten years before Willie's sentence was carried out.

Debbie got word he had been executed and suffered in the process. It was only when he was dead and buried that she realized getting her vengeance didn't set her free like she thought it would. As she put it, "I think I'd finally realized that no punishment—not even the ultimate punishment, the ultimate justice—could ever heal all the wounds."[6]

People who have been betrayed often do not forgive their betrayer because they do not understand how true forgiveness works.

Many people assume, for example, that in order to forgive, the offending party needs to feel sorry, admit guilt, or attempt to reconcile. Saying "I forgive you" is easier when the person admits they have wronged you. But forgiving a person who is no longer in your life or who refuses to admit their actions is tricky.

Debbie realized that if she was ever going to be free, she would have to forgive Willie for what he had done to her, even though he was anything but repentant.

It was hard, but she did it. She didn't have a choice. It was the only way to get delivered from what had happened to her. I'm not sure who originated the line, but is true: "Refusing to forgive is like drinking poison and waiting for the other person to die."

Debbie didn't need that poison in her life.

There was no forgetting what had happened to her, but she did learn to process it. Forgiveness was a part of that—a big part. As she put it in her closing pages:

> The refusal to forgive him always meant that I held on to all my Robert Willie-related stuff—my pain, my shame, my self-pity. That's what I gave up in forgiving him. And it wasn't until I did, that the real healing could even begin.
>
> I was the one who gained…Justice didn't do a thing for me. Forgiveness did. [7]

Today she travels the country and speaks on the power of forgiveness. There's no denying the validity of her testimony.

Trying to Forget Doesn't Work Anyway

Trying to forget hurtful or traumatic experiences often seems easy to anyone who hasn't experienced them. Trying to forget them simply doesn't work. And if we aren't careful, we will feel guilty because we can't forget.

It is inevitable. The longer we sweep things under the rug, the more our pain will pile up and trip us up. It's better to deal with the pile than to ignore it and pretend it isn't there.

I learned this with my dad.

My father fought in the Korean War. For thirteen months, he was on the front lines. My father saw a lot of death and a lot of carnage. He married my mother when he came home, and I didn't come along until six years later. All the same, even as a young child, I can remember the nightmares my dad had.

My father never turned abusive. But he had a lot of excessive anger that he turned inward and other emotions he didn't know how to handle. He suffered mental torment from what he had seen. What made it worse, for years he tried to handle it by trying to forget it.

Although he never denied his military service, he refused to talk about it. He wouldn't bring it up. If someone else mentioned it, he would change the subject. He acted like it had never happened. He didn't keep his medals. He destroyed any pictures from this time in his life.

To him, acting like it never happened was the best way to deal with his haunting memories. He tried to suppress them thinking that would make them go away.

Of course, the opposite happened.

At night his memories would erupt in nightmares. There were other moments when something—a scene from television or even a passing smell—would put him right back on the front. It went on for years.

When I finally was old enough to understand what was happening, I was able to help my dad. I told him he shouldn't deny his memories; he should deal with them. He needed to acknowledge them so that they wouldn't control him any longer.

He tried to talk about the positive things he had experienced during those months and what had come out of his service. He had gone to trade school because of the G.I. Bill. There he learned to be a welder, a trade that allowed him to earn a good living for the rest of his life.

As he did this, the nightmares stopped. He finally admitted, "This is a chapter in my life. I cannot erase it, but I can work through it." Facing it head on was the best thing he could do. It made all the difference.

I remember the day that I secured all of his medals. A friend made a presentation case. My daughter gave it to him for his birthday. Later that day he hung the case on the wall in his home. I sensed for the first time he felt free from the memories of war. As far as I know, he never had another nightmare.

Several years after my friend resigned from our organization and I had time to process it, I got a phone call from an employer where he was applying for a job. When the man said, "We want to ask about one of your former employees," my first thought was, "Here's my chance to get even. I can just tell them, 'You'd be better off if you run him out of town.'"

Yet in my heart, I had forgiven him. I had given up the right to get even. I no longer wanted revenge. I couldn't give him a glowing recommendation and lie to them, but I could honestly answer their questions.

"Yes, he did work here for those years. No, he wasn't fired. He resigned of his own accord."

"Okay, thank you," they said. And then hung up. That was it.

Like my dad, that was the first time in a long time that I felt free. That was the day I realized the wound of what he had done to me no longer hurt. That is when I discovered the difference between a scab and a scar.

When We Know We Can Risk Trusting Again

When we are hurt, healing takes time. The deeper the wound, the longer healing will take. The more severe the injury, the more prominent the scar.

But there's a thing about wounds, especially puncture wounds. When they first happen, they are tender to the touch. We have to be careful with fresh wounds for fear we can open them up again. And if that happens, healing has to start over again.

That is why we leave the bandages on after we receive

stitches—to keep them from getting infected. We protect our wounds for a time to keep them from getting worse. It's all part of the healing process.

Eventually wounds scab over. Then it is safe to take the bandage off. But we need to be careful with the scab so that nothing rips it off or damages it. At first, it will stay sensitive to the touch. We keep it protected and away from things that can reinjure it.

With time, the scabs will fall away, but a scar remains. Usually by the time this happens, the wound is no longer sensitive to the touch. Evidence of the wound, the scar, remains, but the pain is gone. You can touch a wound or a scab and it hurts. You can touch a scar and it doesn't. Both a scab and a scar show a wound occurred. The difference between a wound and a scar is whether it hurts when it is touched. If it still hurts, healing isn't complete. If it doesn't hurt, healing has occurred.

Many of our childhood wounds happened because we didn't realize some things, such as knives and fire aren't toys. Well, relationships aren't toys either. People are not in our lives to be used to get what we want. Mutual respect, love, and forgiveness are important parts of any lasting relationship. That doesn't mean we won't make mistakes and hurt others along the way. Love, however, never hurts others because of carelessness or a complete disregard for the other's feelings and welfare.

A relationship can recover and be reconciled after a betrayal, but it demands the determination of all the parties involved. And it will take time. The wounds caused must be allowed to scab, heal, and turn into scars. We must learn from what happened so that we don't hurt one another carelessly again.

Trust must be earned back.

And it takes more time to heal the wounds of betrayal than

A relationship can recover and be reconciled after a betrayal, but it demands the determination of all the parties involved. And it will take time. Trust must be earned back.

it took to establish the relationship in the first place. In the same way, time is irrelevant when everyone is committed to moving forward together. Love will have to be allowed to fill the void caused by the break. Only then will the relationship have any chance of reconciliation.

Sometimes bonds that have been broken and glued back together will be stronger than the original. Other times they will break again and eventually have to be abandoned. There's no guaranteed process for reconciliation. But if all parties are committed to it, it can be done.

Regardless, we must give ourselves time to heal first. We must get the toxins out and change the bandages until the scab forms. Then we must protect our scabs until they naturally fall off.

Eventually, if we follow the doctor's advice and the scab scars over, we can return to living again, wiser than we were before, less likely to be fooled again, and ready to place ourselves back into God's hands to live the life of fullness He promised us. Then our scars become a testimony that we can survive.

Your Journey to Healing

Forgiveness is not always a one-and-done endeavor. A lot of times our emotions will bring the offense back to mind again and again, and the best way to deal with that is to remind our emotions that we already forgave. We may even need to choose to forgive again.

Here are some things you may want to do if you find yourself struggling with memories reoccurring:

Lift the burden up and give it to God in prayer.

When I was a child, an elderly preacher often said, "Take your burden to the Lord and leave it there." By that he meant we should give God our concern and leave it in His hands—to trust Him to deal with it. Mentally that may be easy to do. Emotionally, however, it is easier said than done.

One thing I have learned works well for those who struggle with this is to go to prayer and imagine lifting that thing up to the Lord with your hands as you would lift a box up to put it on a high shelf.

Tell the Lord you are giving it to Him and don't want to take it back.

Then keep your arms raised until you either feel He has taken it or your arms tire from being raised. Tired arms will remind you that you are not strong enough to carry that burden or unforgiveness any longer.

When you drop your arms, it will be a physical sign to you that you have now forgiven and no longer need to carry that weight.

This isn't some magical ritual. It is a physical act that will remind you that you no longer carry unforgiveness or the burden of what your betrayer did to you. This can be invaluable when the pain or hurt tries to return.

In the Old Testament, the Jews often built monuments as reminders of agreements between families. This simple act of lifting your hands is your way of remembering that the weight of your betrayer's actions are something you no longer need to carry.

Pray short "breath prayers" of blessing on your betrayer.

When you feel the pain of betrayal, it's also good to pray a quick blessing over the offender.

What is it that would turn that person's life and relationship around?

What would reveal the love of God to that person?

What would bring them to true repentance for what they did to you?

Constantly blessing the other person not only releases you further from the hurt you experienced, but God hears prayer! It invites Him into the process and lets His love loose on your betrayer.

You may not feel that your betrayer deserves a blessing or you may not want your betrayer to experience one. But this prayer is more for you than for them. It's a further reminder that you have given them over to God's justice, and God's justice is always administered from His love. There is not greater justice than their repentance and reconciliation with Him.

Truth to Remember

Forgiveness is giving up the right to seek vengeance upon the person who hurt you. It has to do with the past. It does not mean you must open yourself up to be hurt again by that person in the future.

Nine

LOVE

Beloved, never avenge yourselves, but leave it to the wrath of God, for it is written, "Vengeance is mine, I will repay, says the Lord." To the contrary, "if your enemy is hungry, feed him; if he is thirsty, give him something to drink; for by so doing you will heap burning coals on his head." Do not be overcome by evil, but overcome evil with good.

—Romans 12:19-21

Tim was the student pastor at a small church in Oklahoma. He loved what he was doing. When the senior pastor suddenly stepped down because of health issues, the church was in limbo until it could find a new pastor. About the same time, Tim was offered a position as an associate pastor at a growing church in a nearby town. He was torn between going to the slightly larger church for a larger salary or staying and seeing things through with his current congregation.

He met with one of the elders, Bob, to discuss his options.

After Tim laid everything out before him, Bob said, "Tim, you're a gifted teacher, and I know we would be at a loss without you, especially since we really don't have anyone to teach on Sundays until we get a new pastor.

"I'll tell you what—if you will stay, I'll propose to the board that when we get a new pastor, we'll up your salary to match your offer, and then we'll promote you to being an associate pastor. You'll still probably mainly do the youth activities, but at least you can stay with us and keep things going while we interview new candidates. The kids all love you, after all. This would be an awful time to lose you."

It sounded like a good plan. Tim called the other church and turned down the position there. A few weeks later they hired a young man fresh out of Bible school to fill that position.

For the next six months, the church continued with business as usual while the elder board looked for a new pastor. Tim taught regularly to the entire congregation as well as continuing to work with the youth. It was extra duty, but he told his wife it would only be until they found a new pastor. He put in the extra time for the same pay, but everyone seemed so grateful for him being there. He had to admit, he was enjoying it.

When they finally found a senior pastor to take over the pastorate, Tim was ready for things to get back to normal. Then he got a call from the board of elders that they wanted to meet with him. He expected this would be the raise and promotion. He went eagerly.

"Tim, I'm sorry to have to say this," the head elder began, "but one of the requests of the new pastor coming in is that he be able to bring his staff with him, particularly his student pastor."

A sinking feeling came into Tim's gut. He looked at Bob, who seemed to be intently studying his shoes. He wouldn't look up, let alone make eye contact.

"I'm sorry, Tim, but we're a small church. We just don't have room to bring in this new pastor with his staff and still keep you on staff. Of course, you're welcome to remain a member of the church and volunteer with the youth, if you'd like. I know the kids would love to have you stay around. In the meantime, we've arranged to pay you a month's severance while you decide what you're going to do."

"But…" Tim started, looking over at Bob again, who seemed to be melting into his chair. "I met with Bob back in February…I turned down another position to stay…Bob told me—"

"Bob wasn't authorized by the board to make any offers," the head elder cut in. "I'm sorry for any misunderstandings, but it's out of our hands. The new pastor insisted."

Tim looked at Bob again, who was now all but a puddle on the floor. There were so many things he wanted to say.

"But I haven't done anything wrong!"

"I've been faithful to you!"

"I only stayed because you needed me!"

"I filled in, I preached, I met with people who needed prayer!"

Turning to another elder, Tim wanted to say, "William, I went to the hospital when you had your heart attack and stayed and prayed with the family later into the night while you were having emergency surgery. Doesn't any of that mean anything?"

But he held is tongue. He knew any of that would just make things worse. Too dumbfounded to speak, he just stared at them in silence.

"If you need a recommendation or we can help you get resettled in any way, just let us know," the head elder went on. "We're so sorry this had to happen like this, but like I said, it was out of our control."

Tim nodded and looked around the room again. No one but the head elder was willing to meet his eyes. Not able to think of anything else to say, he simply said, "Thank you for letting me know."

Then he got up, numb and defeated, and walked out of the room, out of the church, got into his car, and drove away. In that moment, he was hurting so badly he didn't think he would ever return to that church again.

But he was wrong about that.

The next couple of months were tough for Tim and his young family. Without a salary, not much savings, and scrambling to hang on to their healthcare, they had to decide what they were going to do.

Tim was so decimated by being betrayed by people he considered brothers and sisters, he seriously considered finding a new career. But in the end, he determined that this betrayal didn't need to change who he was and certainly didn't change what he felt was a calling on his life.

So he decided to forgive Bob, the other elders, and his former church so that he could move on. He also determined he would take it a step further. In telling others about what had happened, he would do it in a way that was respectful and courteous. He wouldn't say anything about the promise he had been made, only what he had done and that he had stepped down because the new pastor had staff he was going to bring with him. He would treat it like it was just one of those things and do whatever he could to bless his former employers.

It didn't change the hurt. He still was angry. Every now and then something reminded him of what had happened, but he kept remembering that he forgave them and said a prayer to bless his former church. He acknowledged his anger and did his best to release it, canceling their debt to him and trying to think of ways to bless them.

In short order, Tim got a position at another church that was growing rapidly and needed an associate pastor. He met a new congregation of people and loved stepping up to a new level of responsibility. Tim realized that his time serving and preaching at his former church prepared him for his new responsibility.

A couple of years later, he was asked to come and speak at his old church, and he did so gladly. It was great to hear the stories of how the kids in the student group had grown up and were now off at college, doing well and keeping the faith.

The new pastor greeted him and told him how easy his transition had been because of all Tim had done to fill in after the other pastor had stepped down. He apologized for having replaced him. "That wasn't right," he said. "I should have found a better solution than asking you to leave."

"Don't worry about it," Tim was able to say honestly. "I learned a lot about trusting God that I wouldn't have otherwise. And I feel like I'm in a great place now that I wouldn't be if I'd stayed. I wouldn't have grown as much and have been as assured of my calling. Like Romans 8:28 says, 'for those who love God all things work together for good.' Though it wasn't easy at the time and it didn't make sense to me, I'm better off for it now."

Loving Your Betrayer?

Not all circumstances work out as well as they did for Tim. But after a betrayal, we always are better off doing things God's way. Though we may think otherwise, God doesn't orchestrate such things to try to teach us something. I do believe, however, if we leave things in His hands, He will make a bad situation better if we just follow His precepts.

That's one of the reasons He is called the Redeemer.

When we leave conflicts and issues in His hands, He can make us better than we were. We become stronger, wiser, and deeper. Although we prefer that the betrayal never happened—and I believe God would prefer that as well—our betrayers acted in their God-given freedom. That, however, doesn't nullify God's promises to us if we stay in His ways.

If we are to do that, then forgiving our betrayer is just the first step. On the coattails of that forgiveness is the biblical principle of loving our enemies as Jesus instructed us to do in Luke 6:27-28: "Love your enemies, do good to those who hate you, bless those who curse you, pray for those who abuse you."

I know that may feel like a big order, especially if you haven't forgiven your betrayer yet. I'm not trying to push you too fast. I just want you to have a road map for your healing.

If we want to free ourselves of the stigma of the betrayal, we need to forgive.

If we want to deliver our betrayer into the hands of God for Him to redeem them, we need to start loving them.

These things don't come out of order.

The love you have for a person after a betrayal probably will look and feel different. Just as there are a lot of misunderstandings about our actions after forgiving someone, there are a great deal of misunderstandings about what it means to love a betrayer.

When we leave conflicts and issues in the Redeemer's hands, He can make us better than we were. We become stronger, wiser, and deeper.

As you may already know, the New Testament, written primarily in Greek, has different words to specify different kinds of love. In the English language, we have only the one word.

In the Bible, the Greek word *eros* speaks of romantic love. It is the kind of love two people have for each other when they get married. This is not the word Jesus uses when He tells us to love our enemies.

Another word we translate as love is the word *phileo*. It is the love of friendship. It is used in the word Philadelphia, which is translated "the city of brotherly love." This isn't the word Jesus uses in this passage either.

When he tells us to love our enemies, the word Jesus used is *agape*. This refers to "the love of God," or you could say "loving like God loves." It means wanting the best for that person regardless of what they think of you, how they treat you, or what they have done to you.

It means wanting the best for them, even if they don't want the best for you. It means seeking to bless them even if they are still seeking a way to hurt or deceive you.

It doesn't mean trusting them again. You can want the best for somebody without trusting them.

When I was a young minister I often spoke at our local county jail. Some inmates faced long sentences. Over time, I grew to love several of these young men. I believe many of them had a change of heart after being sentenced to jail. I wanted the best for them and I was willing to help them any way I could. At the same time, I wouldn't give them a key to my home if they were released. Like forgiveness, we give love unconditionally, but trust must be earned or earned again after a betrayal.

Nor does it mean opening yourself up to being hurt again. In many cases, it doesn't even mean you have to see them face-to-face again. It does mean that once you have forgiven—given up your right to seek revenge or to try to penalize them—then you are to love (*agape*) them, meaning you want to see them blessed in the best ways possible. That starts with praying they are reconciled with God.

Forgiveness looks back and releases the offender from future consequences. Love looks forward and does what it can to orchestrate blessings.

It might be best to think of this like a parent's love for an estranged or rebellious adult child. You forgive your son or daughter for whatever happened to drive a wedge between you. You love them by wanting the best for them, even if it means allowing them the time and space to heal. As I wrote in my book *Reaching Your Prodigal: Six Ways to Get Your Son or Daughter Back to God*, love sometimes means refusing to rescue a person and allowing them to face the consequences of their decisions.

To do this, you'll need some emotional distance from what your betrayer did to you.

You'll need to establish a safe place for yourself from which to love.

Loving from a Safe Distance

It wasn't until after I had forgiven my betrayer that I was able to start thinking about how I could love him as Jesus had called me to do. I knew, at that point, the friendship was gone.

Before I could do that, I needed what psychologists Henry Cloud and John Townsend call "emotional distance":

> Emotional distance is a temporary boundary to give
> your heart the space it needs to be safe; it is never a

permanent way of living. People who have been in abusive relationships need to find a safe place to begin to "thaw out" emotionally. Sometimes in abusive marriages the abused spouse needs to keep emotional distance until the abusive partner begins to face his or her problems and becomes trustworthy.

You should not continue to set yourself up for hurt and disappointment. If you have been in an abusive relationship, you should wait until it is safe and until real patterns of change have been demonstrated before you go back. Many people are too quick to trust someone in the name of forgiveness and not make sure that the other person is producing "fruit in keeping with repentance" (Luke 3:8 NIV). To continue to open yourself up emotionally to an abusive or addicted person without seeing true change is foolish. Forgive, but guard your heart until you see sustained change. [8]

While I did not see or interact with my friend, occasionally I heard reports about him. That was tough, because every time I did, it brought back the memories of what had happened. Even though time had dulled the pain, until I was able to forgive him, the reports still stung.

That let me know more healing needed to occur. And it showed me that I needed a bit more space.

It reminded me of advice I once gave to a grieving mother.

There is an intersection near our home where a young woman was killed in an accident with a drunk driver a few years back. A man ran a red light, hit her car, and she died before the paramedics arrived. It was a very sad affair. I remember the grief her parents experienced.

Her friends and family created a small memorial near the

place where she died. They made a small wooden cross, attached photos to it, and planted flowers.

When I recently spoke with the young woman's mother, it surprised me to hear that she had never seen the memorial. "I don't drive down that road anymore," she told me. "It's too painful."

I knew where she lived and I knew where she worked. To avoid that intersection she had to drive four miles out of her way, coming and going, to get around it.

Some people would say that her avoidance of that intersection has gone on long enough. That she's had enough time to grieve the loss of her daughter and forgive the man responsible for the accident.

"She just needs to get over it," they'd say. Other people add, "She hasn't really forgiven the man until she can drive by there and face the reality of what happened."

I strongly disagree.

Why does she need to go back to a place of personal pain before she knows that she is ready? And she is the only one who will know when that is. There probably will be a time when it would be good for her to be able to drive past that intersection again, but that is for her to say, not anyone else.

I also think forgiving the man and working through the grief she feels from losing her daughter are two different things. It's easy to confuse the two, but they are very different and each needs to be processed in its own way.

At the same time, in talking with that mother, I told her, "I think you could live the rest of your life not going by your daughter's memorial, and no one could ever fault you for that. But I think it would be a step of healing if someday you made the decision to take your husband, or your pastor and a friend, and go to that spot. I mean don't just zoom by, but go there and stop and let yourself grieve.

"It's going to be painful, absolutely it's going to be painful. You may want to stop and have a prayer time there. It's going to bring back memories, but it will likely also open up the door to let you heal more, and you won't have to go out of your way every time you leave the house because you're avoiding a place."

In every situation, for every person, it will be different. We will want to test the tenderness of our wounds. Sometimes we will think we are completely healed, but some memory will bring everything back and expose raw feelings again. That is normal. People should have the room to decide whether the wound is still a scab or if it has turned into a scar.

On the other hand, healing can't happen if we run from our pain. There has to be a give-and-take. Every situation is different.

Choosing Love

Loving someone doesn't mean you have to allow them back into your life. At least, they don't need to return in the same way and at the same level they were before the betrayal. This is especially true if their presence causes residual pain.

It doesn't mean you have to be friends again. Nor did forgiving my friend mean that I had to hire him back, even if he produced "fruits in keeping with repentance" (Luke 3:8).

It doesn't mean you have to be reconciled if you were married to the person, especially if they aren't going to change the behavior—the affair, the abuse, refusing to get help for the addiction—that forced you to separate in the first place.

While reconciliation between spouses after an affair is a beautiful thing, every situation is different. You need to determine

I secretively wanted to hear that my betrayer was struggling. That maybe he was having a hard time getting a job or was having problems paying his bills. I still wanted, in some way, to get even.

what is best for you without rushing into things. You have to find a safe place from which to love that person again before you can determine if there is a way to repair the relationship.

That will need some time and help from a pastor or counselor.

After I processed my emotions and forgave my friend, when I heard something about him or was reminded what had happened, the sting of the betrayal lessened. All the same, it was hard not to still inwardly wish ill for him.

I'm being honest here. I didn't want him dead or to be injured in a car wreck. But I secretively wanted to hear that he was struggling. That maybe he was having a hard time getting a job or was having problems paying his bills.

I still wanted, in some way, to get even.

I knew that wasn't right. I knew that wasn't the love of God. So I had to remind myself of what the love of God—what *agape*—looks like. The best place I know for that is in 1 Corinthians 13:4-7. I looked at it in several different Bible translations. Then I read it in *The Message* paraphrase of the Bible:

> Love never gives up.
> Love cares more for others than for self.
> Love doesn't want what it doesn't have.
> Love doesn't strut,
> Doesn't have a swelled head,
> Doesn't force itself on others,
> Isn't always "me first,"
> Doesn't fly off the handle,
> Doesn't keep score of the sins of others,
> Doesn't revel when others grovel,
> Takes pleasure in the flowering of truth,
> Puts up with anything,
> Trusts God always,

Always looks for the best,
Never looks back,
But keeps going to the end.

It is worth taking time to read those words several times, meditating on each line as you do.

As I read this passage to myself over and over again in the weeks that followed, a couple of those lines stuck out to me: "Doesn't keep score of the sins of others," "Takes pleasure in the flowering of truth," and "Always looks for the best."

If I was going to be able to let go of my hurt, I was going to have to let go of my list of things he had done to offend me. I was going to have to clear the scoreboard and start a new game. "The flowering of truth" meant if I heard that he was turning away from his deceit and dealing with the underlining issues that were driving his promiscuous behavior, I would rejoice instead of privately steaming.

If I wanted the best for him, my prayer had to be for him to be healed and reconciled with God. Since I didn't see him at all, the one thing I could do was pray for him daily and ask God to bless and heal him. In a sense, I laid him into the hands of a loving God for Him to do with my friend as He willed.

I found a point of final release when I was fully able to do that without any more malice. I was finally free.

Extending Grace to the Betrayer

One of the hardest steps for anybody who has been betrayed is accepting the grace of God. If God gives grace, His unmerited favor, to my betrayer, can I be mad about it?

It reminds me of the story of the prodigal son, a parable Jesus told (see Luke 15:11-32). After the wayward son wasted his inheritance and finally came home, his father welcomed him and prepared a feast for him. His father celebrated his return.

When the older brother heard what was happening, he got angry. Why celebrate the one who had gone astray when he had been faithful to his father? Why make a big deal about a betrayer coming to his or her senses and coming back to God rather than celebrating the one who had been faithful?

Because the prodigal was lost, and now he was found. He was home again.

The elder brother—like many of us who have been betrayed—never left home. We always had the comfort of being with the Father and the bounty of His blessings. We were never outside of the fold.

For us, we need to remember that grace welcomes home the betrayer. Grace prepares a feast, celebrates the betrayer's return, and doesn't sulk because of the attention a repentant betrayer receives. Grace seeks the best for the betrayed and the betrayer.

When you understand and embrace grace, you are free to love and trust again.

Your Journey to Healing

God's love functions best from a place of stability, just like the house built on the rock that Jesus spoke about in Matthew 7:24-27. That means sometimes we need to fill ourselves before we can give to others. Here are a few ways to do that:

Meditate on Scriptures about love.

First Corinthians 13 is, of course, a great passage to read and meditate on each phrase. The Sermon on the Mount in Matthew 5–7 is another, as is the book of 1 John. Pick a passage and read it every day for one month. Think about it throughout the day. (Don't be dogmatic about doing it. If you miss a day or a couple, it's no big deal; just pick it up again where you left off the next day.)

Write different verses on sticky notes and put them on your refrigerator door or bathroom mirror. If you're an artist (or even if you aren't), turn the verses that speak to your heart the most into something you can hang on your wall.

Our physical bodies require us to eat every day. Food is essential to life. In the same way, our spiritual lives need daily nourishment. You need daily insight from the Bible. That is why Jesus said that we need to feed our souls with the "every word that comes from the mouth of God" (Matthew 4:4).

Respond to harsh words with loving ones.

It can be shocking when someone speaks harshly or cruelly to us, especially from our betrayer or their friends. It often leaves us wanting to strike back with the same venom. When you aren't in the fire of such a verbal attack, think about how you can respond with kindness instead of malice. You don't need a bunch of different responses. One or two will do. You could say something like: "Thank you for sharing." "I'm sorry you feel that way." Or don't answer at all.

The point isn't to have a snappy answer to put them in their place. You respond to dissipate the anger and give yourself space to reply in kindness rather than with animosity.

Again, don't make yourself a doormat and just give in. It takes some thought and practice to get it right. You may want to practice responses with a friend or counselor. Know how to stand your ground in a loving way for the respect you deserve. There is no more powerful example of love than doing this like Jesus did in the face of His accusers.

Truth to Remember

God commands us to love our enemies. Loving people comes from a place of strength and stability. It never involves accepting wrong, especially at your expense. *No* can be a powerful love word.

Ten

HEALING

Forgiveness must be immediate, whether or not a person asks for it.
Trust must be rebuilt over time. Trust requires a track record.

—Rick Warren

'm sure you've heard the story of Joseph and his coat of many colors. How at the age of seventeen he boasted to his older brothers and parents about his dream of them bowing down to him. How his brothers grew jealous of this oldest son of their father's more cherished wife. How they wanted to kill him and throw his carcass into a pit, and how, at the last minute, Joseph's oldest brother, Reuben, convinced them to spare his life and sell him to a traveling caravan instead.

I can only imagine how deeply their betrayal cut into Joseph's heart.

For the next thirteen years, Joseph had to decide what to do with that pain. And his bondage wasn't metaphorical. He spent his time as an actual slave and then in prison for a sexual assault he never committed.

It wasn't just his brothers that betrayed him, but his employer's wife betrayed him as well. When Joseph refused her sexual advances toward him, she lied, accused him of trying to rape her, and had her husband put him in prison.

Joseph had to decide what he was going to do with his feelings toward his family, his employer, and God. For the most part, we don't know Joseph's thoughts or emotions. We do know he had plenty of time to process his feelings. And there is another fact we know. Joseph never wavered in his faith in God or his belief that one day everything would work out for his good. Joseph is one of the few major characters in the Old Testament about whom nothing negative is said.

As a result, in the midst of the worst of human conditions—as a slave and as a prisoner—Joseph prospered.

Joseph had a promise revealed to him in a dream as a young man. It was a dream that his brothers one day would bow down to him. And it was that dream that caused his brothers to betray him.

But Joseph knew he had a God-given ability to interpret dreams, which, in the end, was the thing that brought him to Pharaoh's attention. That was when Pharaoh released Joseph from prison and made him the second most powerful authority in Egypt.

When the famine hit and Joseph's dream came true—his brothers came to Egypt seeking food to take back to the family—Joseph was able to deal with it because he had forgiven his brothers long ago. He sincerely loved them. That is the reason he was not going to let them or the rest of his family go hungry. He wished the best for them and would bless them in spite of themselves if he had to.

But he still had a question.

Could he trust them?

The end of Joseph's story in the book of Genesis goes into great detail about how he hid himself from his brothers and tested their loyalty to their family. He kept a safe distance and spoke to them through an interpreter. He made one brother stay and sent the other nine back, asking them to return with his younger brother, Benjamin, to prove themselves. He returned the money they used to purchase grain to see if they would be honest about getting the grain for free.

Would they choose to keep the money over their imprisoned brother as they had done with Joseph?

How would they respond when they were falsely accused of being spies?

How would they respond if they were asked to give up another brother to save their own lives?

When Judah, one of Joseph's brothers, offered to be a slave in order for Benjamin to return to his father and not be grieved over the loss of a second son, Joseph saw that his brothers had changed and had repented of what they had done to him. He no longer needed to distance himself from them. That is when he took off his disguise and told them who he was.

They were astonished and told him how sorry they were for what they had done earlier in his life.

Joseph told them he had never been out of God's hands and that through what they had done, God was now using Joseph to save the known world from the monstrous famine they were facing. Afraid that, after their father's death, Joseph would use his power to seek revenge against them, he told them instead, "you meant evil against me, but God meant it for good" (Genesis 50:20).

Can we turn our betrayal stories around in a similar way?

Can we also take our lives back and learn to trust again, for the benefit of all involved? I think we can.

Trust Issues

The Bible tells us we should forgive others. The Great Commandment is to love God and our neighbor. There is no requirement in the Bible, however, to trust anyone but God.

Trust is not among the qualities of love in 1 Corinthians 13. It does tell us, "Love bears all things, believes all things, hopes all things, endures all things" (1 Corinthians 13:7), but when it says "believe all things," I think that means we are to take people at their word until they prove unreliable. That may be a form of trust, but I think it is more hope.

Hope they are telling the truth, but don't bet your well-being on it. Who we trust in our lives is up to us.

Trust is the currency of relationships. It is the basis upon which we let people into our lives. When a person is betrayed, the greatest casualty is that trust. It is also the most difficult thing to get back.

If there is any hope for reconciliation, we must be very decisive in how we go about it.

We build trust casually as a relationship forms. We explore similarities and get to know each other. As trust grows, we share more about who we are.

If that trust is violated in a major way, as it is in a betrayal, rebuilding that trust needs to be pursued more formally. If we want to rebuild it after a betrayal—if we really desire restoration—the more specific we can be about it, the better for both parties.

Avoid Common Mistakes

When a person is betrayed, they tend to make one of two mistakes.

The first is to think that forgiveness means to forget and return to the relationship as if nothing had ever happened—to restore trust without expecting the other person to do anything to earn that trust back.

The second is to be skeptical about trusting anyone ever again. When this happens, mistrust is often generalized.

"After what happened, I'm never going to trust a preacher again."

"All politicians and lawyers are crooks."

"You need to watch your employees like a hawk."

"Men! They're all scoundrels!"

"I don't trust anyone in my family."

"You can never trust a woman." And so forth.

After my betrayal, I fell a little into both of these traps. First of all, I accepted my friend's repentance at face value. While he may have been sincere about it at the time, he didn't stay repentant. He returned to the same behavior a short time later. He even used what I had told him about how I discovered his deceptions to try to keep from getting caught again.

He did agree to go to counselling and get help, but made excuse after excuse to skip out on those meetings.

The ground rules I set for restoring trust in him were too lax. I didn't build any kind of review process to make sure he was staying faithful to his promise to end his promiscuous behavior.

As Cloud and Townsend put it in *Boundaries*: "Forgiveness has to do with the past. Reconciliation and boundaries have to do with the future. Limits guard my property until someone has repented and can be trusted to visit again."[9] I should have made a more formal agreement that we could have checked from time to time to be sure he was working to earn my trust back.

On the other hand, I stuffed my feelings and, without realizing it, began to distrust anyone who didn't take my side of the betrayal.

I easily could have projected that at work, perhaps pulling the long-distance bills and other reports for other employees from time to time to see if I found anything suspicious. Luckily I didn't fall into that pit, though I know bosses who have.

It would be easy to obsess about such things.

This happens when you are not direct and specific about what happened. When we don't deal with it openly, it leaves all kinds of room for misinterpretation and misunderstandings, which is why it is good to be very specific when setting ground rules.

Put Your Rebuilding Plan in Writing

As we recover from betrayal—even after we have forgiven and found a way to love that person again as God wants us to do—it's perfectly natural to come up with some precise guidelines to protect you or anyone you know from being hurt in the same way again.

In fact, determining good ground rules is an expression of our healing process. It gives us behaviors to observe—and behaviors to avoid—to make it safe to trust each other again.

Such ground rules really come from asking ourselves, "What do I need to be assured is happening to be able to trust again?"

Determining good ground
rules is an expression
of our healing process.
It gives us behaviors to
observe—and behaviors
to avoid—to make it safe
to trust each other again.

This list will be different for each relationship—the closer the relationship, the more formal this process should be.

If it is a work relationship, if could be done under the guidance of the human resources department. If it is a marriage, it should be done with a counselor of some kind. It should be treated like a contract that both parties sign in agreement.

Here are a few guidelines for creating these ground rules:

Your ground rules should be action oriented.

"You need to be nicer to me" is too vague. It leaves too much to interpretation. "Look me in the eyes and give me your full attention when we are speaking" is much easier to both do and verify.

List everything.

Don't beat around the bush. "I want you to tell me every time you run into the woman you had an affair with" is not out of line. It could also be things like, "I want you to look at your laptop only in the dining room or family room when other people are around."

"We need to install a program to record your online activity."

"You shouldn't work past 5:00 p.m. at the office anymore. If you need to work more hours, go in earlier in the morning."

Your ground rules need to be verifiable.

Here are some examples:

"Your counselor will agree to call me if you ever miss a meeting."

"You will turn on the GPS on your phone whenever you travel and promise to keep it with you."

"All of our bank accounts should be in both of our names."

"Give me the login information for all of your credit cards."

"We will have an outside firm audit our books every year after taxes."

Your ground rules shouldn't just be restrictive.

"Once a week we'll go on a date together, and we will get away for a romantic weekend every quarter."

"We agree to go to counselling together for ten sessions."

"You'll call me at lunch every day and we'll talk for five minutes."

It is healthy to set goals, such as getting away. If, however, it is handled like a legal contract, love cannot flourish.

Set a schedule to revisit and revise this list after a few months. These ground rules should change the rhythms at home or work or in your social life that may have facilitated growing apart. You need to move other things out of the way so that you can be together to rebuild.

This, again, will take time.

The more specific and definite you are about it, the easier it will be to see your progress and feel hopeful about your future together.

This isn't an opportunity to punish the other person. You should focus on rebuilding trust. It might even be good to have a chart or a whiteboard where you can record when these happen for reference. Some of the things on your list will be smaller and easier to do; others may require more of a life change and negotiation.

"I'm so embarrassed by what happened, I want us to move to another state where we can start over."

"I want a clause in my contract that says I will get a certain amount of money if you ever sell the company."

"I'd like you to put those promises in writing."

I know sometimes this can seem like it is going a bit too far, especially to the unfaithful person in the relationship. "She wants to check up on me at all hours of the day," one husband told me. "He wants me to take a picture together with whoever is with me at lunch," a wife complained to me.

Let me say a brief word to the betrayer. If you really want to reconcile, then you are going to need to put up with some uncomfortable requests. Remember, after all, these are for the other person's reassurance and rebuilding trust with them, not for your convenience. At least a little of this comes with the territory because of your betrayal. If you really want to reconcile, you need to do what is necessary to rebuild trust.

If you, as the offender, want to be trusted again, then you must be transparent enough to continually prove you are trustworthy.

You need to realize as well that you can't completely undo what you did, you can only facilitate the healing. You can't undo a car accident, but you can recover from it. If there were physical injuries, there will be a scar that remains. You can't overreact in the process of that injury scabbing over and becoming a scar.

If you were unfaithful to your spouse, then your spouse has the right to question anything you do, anywhere you go, anyone you're with, and you can't get upset about it. You have to give your spouse the right to say, "I'm not comfortable with you doing that," and be willing to honor him or her by saying, "Then I won't do it."

Don't get defensive. That's no way to rebuild trust.

On the other hand, this is not license for the betrayed partner to smother the betrayer in requirements. It's not handing over control of their lives. Such things might make a betrayer feel they are better off on their own, which isn't the desired result.

Besides, this really isn't about checks and balances as much as it is building new openness and honesty with one another. This is another reason it is good to have the help of a counselor who will mediate disagreements so that everyone can be on the same page and know their part in healing the relationship.

When You Can't Reconcile but Still Need to See Each Other Regularly

This probably happens more when marriages end and there are children involved than anywhere else. Sometimes you may still attend the same church or still have to work with your betrayer. Your betrayer may have kids in the same school or play the same sports.

Reconciliation isn't always possible, and as we've already discussed, it isn't always the best or safest option. Sometimes the other person will be completely unrepentant but still have visitation rights with your kids and you will have to see them—sometimes even with their partners in betrayal—when they are dropped off or picked up.

Such legal arrangements tend to be very general unless you can prove there are safety or well-being concerns that need to be taken into account.

You might remember Joyce from a couple chapters back whose husband got abusive when he drank. She requested that he not drink when he had the kids nor would he have alcohol in his home when they were there. Such things can be hard to control, and you may need to seek legal advice.

The bottom line in such situations is you need to ask for what you want and use the word *no* when you don't feel comfortable about the situation.

I know one woman whose husband wanted the whole family

to spend Christmas together—ex-spouses, kids, and his new live-in girlfriend. I let her know she had every right to opt out of such invitations. She needed to calmly and rationally refuse the offer.

On the other hand, betrayal doesn't define the whole person. A man could be unfaithful to his wife and still spend quality time with his kids. A woman could have an emotional affair and still be a wonderful, loving mother.

While it's arguable that a good mother or father wouldn't be unfaithful to their mate, if there's no reconciling the relationship, you still have to act for the benefit of all, especially the kids who shouldn't be expected to take sides.

We shouldn't be pouring out our hurt on them or subjecting them to everything we think is wrong with the other parent. This is where forgiveness and love should again guide our actions. We need to really keep our emotions in check in such situations. It's never easy, which is why it's so important to walk with God through these things. It's best for our kids to have both parents in their lives with a minimal amount of strife. They need to know the love of both parents.

Your Solid Place to Stand

None of this is easy. That especially is true if your identity and self-worth are all tied up in it. As I've said before, though, we can't let being betrayed define us. We need to be defined by something more solid than our relationships. Only when we live on that solid ground can we give the best, especially in an uncertain world.

We must cling to that which is solid and trustworthy. We must hold tight to that which will last. Jesus described it in this way:

"Everyone then who hears these words of mine and does them will be like a wise man who built his house on the rock. And the rain fell, and the floods came, and the winds blew and beat on that house, but it did not fall, because it had been founded on the rock. And everyone who hears these words of mine and does not do them will be like a foolish man who built his house on the sand. And the rain fell, and the floods came, and the winds blew and beat against that house, and it fell, and great was the fall of it" (Matthew 7:24-27).

I know it's a simple illustration, but a lot of times I think of trusting God and living by the teachings of Scripture as being like getting to a location using a GPS navigation device. I remember when I got my first GPS in our car, I wasn't used to following directions coming from a machine: "Go left here, turn right here. In five hundred feet, merge right. Your destination is ahead on the left." I always worried that I would miss a turn and have to turn around in a place I didn't know.

And, of course, I eventually did miss a turn. There was an accident and the police were directing traffic away from where I was supposed to turn. As I went straight and off route, I thought I'd have to stop and reprogram my destination. Instead I heard my GPS say, "Recalibrating." In a few moments it gave me new directions to get me where I needed to go.

The grace of God is like that for our lives. Sometimes we make bad decisions and get off course. Sometimes there are accidents. And sometimes other people do inexplicable things and derail our lives.

That's not the point at which we should turn off our life GPS, pull over to the side of the road, and just stay there feeling sorry for ourselves. Maybe we need to do that for a time to reorient ourselves and get over the emotions of the setback, but we don't want to end our journeys there because of a bump in the road or a flat tire.

We need to let God recalibrate our way forward. This may lead us to a slower road, maybe a rougher road, maybe a longer road, or maybe a more scenic route, who knows? But if we are willing to keep moving, we can still get to where we need to go.

I think there are times in our life when we see God's plan for where He wants us to go, and we assume God is going to take us on the easy, short, get on the freeway, no toll roads, direct route. But in my experience, that rarely happens.

Instead life happens. People get in the way and sometimes even betray us. We live in a war zone of contending desires, egos, and hurts. Doing the right things is not always the easiest or most desirable of things to do.

We need to be ready for the storms, and the only way to do that is to keep our homes built on the Rock.

I wish I could promise you nobody will ever betray you again. But I can't. Mishaps happen, people hurt, and hurt people have a tendency to hurt others.

Being betrayed once won't keep you from being betrayed again. But that is the price we pay for opening ourselves up to relationships and loving others. My hope is that by successfully processing the hurt of your betrayal, if it happens again, you'll be in a more solid place to recover the next time.

I know that's how it's been for me. Business often means competing with others and needing the help of people. People are fallible, and other people have betrayed me in my life.

Having processed the pain of my friend's betrayal made me

We must be willing to pour out our frustrations, pain, and even our anger to God so that He can replace them with His grace and love.

better. It enabled me to weather those storms. And it helped me help others rebuild their houses after their collapse—for those who were willing, anyway.

The foundation of all other trust must be our trust that God is good and wants the best for us. Like Joseph, even when things look horrible, we must dig our foundations into Him all the deeper.

We must be willing to pour out our frustrations, pain, and even our anger to Him so that He can replace them with His grace and love. We may not emerge from prison to take our place as a ruler over people as Joseph did, but God does have a destination in mind for us. It is a place of abundant and joyful life.

No matter what happens to us, we can take that life back from people who selfishly hurt us or try to do us harm. Betrayal need not define the rest of our days. Our trust in God and walking in His healing ways should.

A Visual Illustration

If you are like me, sometimes it helps if I can see something that represents the brokenness that I experienced.

Recently I saw an unusual piece of pottery. It was a navy-blue bowl. But there was something unique about it. The bowl obviously was broken—shattered, in fact—but an artist put it back together with what appeared to be gold.

I learned that the pottery was a piece of kintsugi, a Japanese art of fixing broken pottery with a special epoxy that is dusted with gold. The ancient art form has its roots in the belief that regret should come from something valuable being wasted. So, the Japanese found a way to put broken pottery back together with a compound covered with gold.

As a result, the repaired pieces tend to be more beautiful than the original. Instead of hiding the cracks and flaws, the potter drew attention to them. He celebrated what the pieces became after being shattered.

The same is true of people betrayed by others. We try to hide our pain. Instead, something beautiful occurs when we are honest and forgiving. When we allow the Golden Rule of "do to others as you would have them do to you" (see Matthew 7:12) to govern our relationships in the future, we discover our deepest value.

For me, I have a small piece of kintsugi pottery in my office. It is a visual reminder that betrayal caused me to experience brokenness, but my Lord didn't leave me there. As I followed His leadership, He put my life back together in a more beautiful way.

You may be like me. You need something to see as a reminder of God's work in your life. A search on the internet will show you small, inexpensive pieces you can purchase. Put it where you regularly will view it. And remember that it is not the repaired piece of pottery that is valuable—it is the new you.

The Day I Realized I Got My Life Back

I can still remember the day that I realized my joy in life was back.

I can't remember why, but for some reason I parked my car in the driveway instead of the garage the night before. Winter was coming to an end and spring was starting to bud in the trees.

It was time to go to work, so I walked outside and crossed our lawn to get to my car. Then something struck me.

The sun was shining. The chill of winter was gone. And I heard something I couldn't remember hearing for some time.

The birds were singing.

When was the last time I noticed the birds were singing?

My mind traveled back through my memories. It had been years.

In fact, I couldn't remember a day like this since those government agents walked into my office. I couldn't remember a single time I had stopped to listen to the birds since then—since I'd walked through the pain and anger that I'd experienced the day I first realized my good friend had betrayed me.

I stopped for a moment and wondered, "Had I been so closed off all of these years, I hadn't even noticed the beauty of life going on around me? That I hadn't even heard the birds sing?"

In that moment, I realized I had been.

I could always say, "God is good" through the previous years, but this was the first time in some time I realized I could also say, "Life is good." That it was good to be alive, feel the sun on my face, and be grateful for all God had given me in life.

Betrayal can take all of that away, but God will give it back if you walk with Him through healing the hurt and pain of it.

There is better on the other side.

I cannot promise you that your healing will follow the same course mine did. Some journeys will be longer. Some will have to deal with more of your childhood and past; others will have to be processed while the betrayer is still in your life every day.

Every journey will be unique. At the same time, I believe we all go through a similar process of grieving the loss of innocence we feel when betrayed. We all will struggle to get back on the road to trusting again.

But I do believe that if you follow the pattern laid out in these pages, there will come a day when you will hear the birds singing again. You will again feel the sun on your face, recognize that it's spring, and be glad you're alive to experience God's goodness.

I promise you that day will come.

I look forward to hearing the story of your healing journey.

Your Journey to Healing

While forgiveness is often marked as a one-time "letting go," rebuilding trust requires consistent and repeated actions. Perhaps you could think of it as building a bridge across a river or ravine: each person needs to build from their side to meet in the middle.

What does the other person really need to do to regain your trust? What actions will let you know they're not yet ready to build this bridge with you?

Make lists.

Answer some of the following questions in your journal:

- What boundaries do you need to set to protect your safety and well-being?
- What boundaries do you need to set to protect the safety and well-being of anyone else involved (your children, for example)?
- What would make you feel more loved and appreciated?
- What things would you want to be assured of not happening again?
- What assurances does the other person need to make so you can be sure they are continuing to work on their recovery?
- What are positive ways you can love your betrayer even if there's no way to rebuild trust with them?

List your responses to any other questions that occur to you.

Don't keep moving the finish line.

While it's okay to change or renegotiate certain things from time to time, be sure you aren't creating expectations that are unrealistic or unreasonable. This usually only happens when we aren't honest about our expectations in the first place.

If you do need to change or add something, be willing to explain yourself and allow the other person to add something to their list as well.

Let us know your healing story.

We want to know how God used this book in your life and how He has helped you heal. Send us your healing story at mystory@beyondbetrayalbook.com.

Truth to Remember

The path back to trust isn't easy, but it is of immeasurable value. Trust is the currency of relationships, and relationships bring joy to life. Nothing should take that away from you.

....

BIBLE PASSAGES WITH THE POWER TO HELP YOU HEAL

Throughout my life, in good times and bad, I've always found it helpful to meditate on Bible stories and different Scriptures to help me heal and stay grounded. Here are several passages I found helpful in processing my pain and recovering from betrayal.

The story of Joseph

- Genesis 37 and 39–50

The story of David, Uriah, and Bathsheba

- 2 Samuel 11–12

Various Psalms of lament

- Psalm 27

- Psalm 41
- Psalm 51
- Psalm 55
- Psalm 89
- Psalm 125

The importance of forgiveness

- Matthew 6:14-15
- Mark 11:25

Peter's betrayal and reconciliation

- Luke 22:54-62; John 21:15-19

The nature of God's love

- 1 Corinthians 13

DISCUSSION GUIDE

Session One

Read chapters 1-2 in preparation for discussing the following questions.

1. In the introduction, Phil Waldrep expressed some of the questions people who are betrayed ask. Which of these questions have you asked and why?

2. Read 2 Samuel 15:7-12 and 2 Samuel 15:30-31. David experienced betrayal from Absalom, his son, and from a trusted advisor, Ahithophel. Why do you think Absalom and Ahithophel betrayed David? What motives do you see in the person who betrayed you?

3. Read Psalm 41:8-10. What emotions do you think David felt as a result of the betrayal? How have you experienced the same feelings?

4. Before David expressed his pain in Psalm 41:9, he acknowledged his own sin in Psalm 41:4. What are some sins that are easy to commit when someone betrays you? Why is it hard for a betrayed person to confess and forsake these sins?

5. It took Phil Waldrep twenty years before he was able to discuss his pain. Why do you think it is hard for people to discuss in a healthy, healing way their betrayal? Why do you think time makes it easier?

6. One way that betrayal occurs is when we are part of a larger group (a youth group, congregation, group of employees,

a citizen) that has been betrayed. Sometimes it is easier to discuss these betrayals because others are part of the group and feel our pain. Have you ever experienced a betrayal because you were part of a group? How did it make you feel?

7. How do/did the following steps to healing from betrayal help you process the betrayal?

   • Admit you've been hurt.
   • Give yourself permission to be angry.
   • Don't tell yourself, "I've got this."
   • Stop trying to be super-Christian.

8. How do you respond to this statement: "We cannot let the betrayal determine our worth"?

9. Being betrayed often forces us to focus on the pain and forget the blessings in our life. What are some of the blessings you have that, despite your pain, demonstrate God's goodness to you?

Session Two

Read chapters 3-4 in preparation for discussing the following questions.

1. Ask anyone to name a betrayer and almost everyone will mention Judas. Before he betrayed Jesus, others viewed Judas as a faithful follower of Christ. As a disciple, what are some of the miraculous things Judas experienced? What are some things Jesus said that should have caused Judas to see His message as spiritual and not political?

2. Read Matthew 27:1-5. Why do you think Judas changed his mind about his betrayal? How do you think he felt when the chief priests and elders no longer cared about him (v. 4)? Do you think he felt betrayed? Why or why not?

3. Although the Bible gives us no indication how Jesus or the disciples would have responded if Judas had sought their forgiveness, why do you think Judas committed suicide instead of asking for their forgiveness? How do you think Jesus would have responded? How do you think the disciples would have?

4. How do you respond to this statement: "Betrayers don't just betray you—they betray themselves"? If you agree, why do we blame ourselves for the betrayal?

5. Read 2 Samuel 11. As you do, try to see the story through the eyes of Uriah, Bathsheba's husband. Did Uriah do anything wrong? What did he do right?

6. While living, Uriah didn't know about the adultery. Imagine for a moment Uriah survived the battle and later learned of the adultery. What emotions do you think he might have felt? Why? How would the powerful position of King David affect his reactions? How do you feel when your betrayer is in a position of power?

7. How do you react to this statement: "Shame is a powerful emotion"? Why do people who are betrayed feel shame? How can shame prevent healing the emotions from a betrayal?

8. How can a healthy church and supportive friends help you walk through betrayal? What are some specific things they can do to help you emotionally and spiritually?

Session Three

Read chapters 5-6 in preparation for discussing the following questions.

1. Why do you think people want to keep denying that someone has betrayed them? What does admitting the betrayal force us to do?

2. How does the community around us (family members, coworkers, friends) affect our willingness to accept betrayal? Why do you think people around us are quicker to deny the betrayal than we are? How does their denial of the betrayal prompt you to continue denying it too?

3. Phil Waldrep wrote, "The pain of betrayal equals the level of trust times the amount of investment." How is that confirmed in your betrayal?

4. Blaming others is a common reaction when we are betrayed. Honestly, who are some of the people you have blamed and why?

5. Read Genesis 3:8-13. Why do you think Adam blamed God (v. 12)? Why are we prone to blame God for our betrayal?

6. Why do you think we isolate ourselves from people when we are betrayed? How have some relationships in your life changed due to betrayal? What are some ways you form new relationships?

7. How has your church helped you during your betrayal? What are some ways you can connect with new people in your church?

Session Four

Read chapters 7-8 in preparation for discussing the following questions.

1. What are some unhealthy ways we express our emotions? What are some healthy ways we can express them?

2. Read Exodus 32:15-20. Why do you think Moses expressed his anger the way he did? Was his anger justified? Why or why not?

3. Read Ephesians 4:26-27. What are some ways we can be angry and "sin not"? What are some steps we can take to make sure we don't allow our anger to build?

4. Why is it healthy to avoid telling everyone the details of our betrayal? What are some guidelines to follow to govern our conversations?

5. Read Hebrews 12:15. What do you think the writer meant by a "root of bitterness"? How can a bitter spirit affect us? Our relationships? Our family?

6. Phil Waldrep encouraged us to journal our thoughts and feelings. Why is writing our feelings better than verbally expressing them to others? What are some creative ways you found to vent your feelings?

7. What role does prayer play in healing our hurts? How has prayer affected you since your betrayal?

8. Read Matthew 7:12 and Matthew 22:39. How important is a healthy respect for yourself in relationships? How does a lack of self-worth negatively affect us?

9. What are some misconceptions you had about forgiveness before reading chapter 8? How important do you think biblical forgiveness is in your journey to healing?

Session Five

Read chapters 9-10 in preparation for discussing the following questions.

1. Why do we like revenge when we have been hurt? Why is it difficult to sincerely love those who betrayed us?

2. Read Luke 23:32-43. How did the forgiveness of Jesus affect the criminals crucified with Him? Why do you think Jesus was able to forgive?

3. Why are distance and boundaries important in recovering from betrayal? What are some ways you can practice them in your life?

4. What are some ways you can move beyond your betrayal and start healing? What are some places or events you need to encounter to continue healing? Who are some people who can help you take those steps?

5. Read Luke 15:11-32. How did the father and the older brother respond differently? Why do you think they responded the way they did? How does the father's reaction give you a model to follow?

6. Read Genesis 45:1-15. How did Joseph's response affect his brothers? How can your love and forgiveness affect your betrayers?

7. Phil Waldrep described the practice of putting broken pottery together using gold to create something useful and

beautiful. How do you think God can use your betrayal to make something beautiful and useful?

8. What are five things you would like to see God help you do to continue your journey of getting beyond betrayal?

ENDNOTES

1. Simplified from Merriam-Webster's Collegiate Dictionary, 11th ed. (Springfield, MA: Merriam-Webster, Incorporated, 2003), s.v., "betray."

2. Randi Gunther, PhD, "How Infidelity Causes Post Traumatic Stress Disorder: Healing from Betrayal," *Psychology Today*, September 29, 2017, www.psychologytoday.com/us/blog/rediscovering-love/201709/how-infidelity-causes-post-traumatic-stress-disorder.

3. "An Outline History of the Twelve Apostles," *The Open Bible* (Nashville, TN: Thomas Nelson Publishers, 1975), 1246.

4. "Holmes and Rahe Stress Scale," *Wikipedia* (last edited: May 7, 2019), https://en.wikipedia.org/wiki/Holmes_and_Rahe_stress_scale.

5. Todd Kashdan and Robert Biswas-Diener, "The Right Way to Get Angry," *Greater Good Magazine,* October 20, 2014, https://greatergood.berkeley.edu/article/item/the_right_way_to_get_angry.

6. Debbie Morris, *Forgiving the Dead Man Walking* (Grand Rapids, MI: Zondervan Publishing House, 1998), 174.

7. Ibid., 249-50, 251.

8. Henry Cloud and John Townsend, *Boundaries: When to Say Yes, How to Say No to Take Control of Your Life* (Grand Rapids, MI: Zondervan Publishing House, 1992), 36-37.

9. Ibid., 263.